Praise for *LEAVING TH*

"I thoroughly enjoyed *Leaving the Dese[...]* an excellent description of the basic metaphysics and psychology of *A Course in Miracles* and its practical application in daily life, written in a clear conversational style."
—Jon Mundy, PhD, author of *Living A COURSE IN MIRACLES*

"Written with humor and courageous self-disclosure, Pauline Edward's *Leaving the Desert* is a delight. Through sharing her own exploration—her commitment and her doubts—she addresses all the major topics covered in *A Course in Miracles* with precision and clarity. For new students as well as veterans of the Course, her overview of its purpose and methodology is excellent. Her adroit sprinkling of personal anecdotes enlivens and clarifies her path (and ours) and her honesty allows the book to be a comforting companion to those seeking to engage more artfully with this life-changing practice. You will read this book with a smile of recognition and gratitude."
—Carol Howe, author of *Never Forget To Laugh: Personal Recollections of Bill Thetford, Co-scribe of A COURSE IN MIRACLES, Healing the Hurt Behind Addictions and Compulsive Behaviors,* and *Homeward To an Open Door, Exploring Major Principles of A COURSE IN MIRACLES*

"In *Leaving the Desert: Embracing the Simplicity of A COURSE IN MIRACLES,* Pauline Edward shares her intimate quest both to fully comprehend the Course's fundamental principles despite the ego's formidable resistance and to apply its unique forgiveness in her daily life. *Leaving the Desert* will inspire Course newbies and veterans alike with its profound, comprehensive understanding and specific examples fearlessly and generously drawn from the classroom of the author's life. The book is a must for anyone sincerely committed to healing their mind of the idea of competing interests at the root of human suffering and thereby inviting the deeply comforting memory of our true, universal nature."
—Susan Dugan, author of *Extraordinary Ordinary Forgiveness*

"Pauline Edward delivers the concepts of *A Course in Miracles* elegantly and uncompromisingly, and with an undeniably gifted style. This book is wonderful. It offers a deep and much-needed exploration of the core message of *A Course in Miracles*. It comes from profound guidance, and places the reader at the altar of Truth. *Leaving the Desert* is a must-read for any student of the Course, or any person seeking enlightenment."
—Robyn Busfield, author of *Forgiveness is the Home of Miracles*

"Although able to stand on its own, *Leaving the Desert* picks up where Pauline Edward's spiritual journey left off in her previous book *Making Peace with God*. *Leaving the Desert* presents an overview of the central themes of *A Course in Miracles* in the context of the ongoing personal story of the author. The chapter I most liked (which is to say, the chapter I found the most special) was the chapter on Specialness. That chapter is an excellent exposé of the true nature of specialness. And it is a chapter I am sure to read over many times. This world is a desert. And a desert is a desert and nothing more. The thing to do with a desert is to leave it. But to do that, you'll certainly want to read this book to help guide you on your way."
—Alexander Marchand, author of *The Universe Is a Dream*

"*Leaving the Dessert* is a beautiful work filled with treasures of truth, touching honesty and breakthrough experiences with which students of *A Course in Miracles* are sure to relate. It is a deep expression of the author's personal journey with the Course and her devotion to the spiritual life and to Jesus. It is a comforting place to fall, to feel understood, to feel and know you are not alone.

I am blessed to have had the opportunity to use my gift to pass along words of guidance to Pauline from our beloved older brother and teacher, J, in her moments of need. I will remain forever grateful for having had these opportunities to stand in the presence of the great Love that is our natural inheritance. Thank you Pauline for this incredible gift of you and your book."
—Lisa LaJoie, Channeller

LEAVING
THE
DESERT

LEAVING THE DESERT

Embracing the Simplicity of
A Course in Miracles

Pauline Edward

Desert Lily Publications
Montreal, Canada

V1.06

Library and Archives Canada Cataloguing in Publication

Edward, Pauline, 1954-
Leaving the desert: embracing the simplicity of a Course in Miracles/ Pauline Edward.

Includes bibliographical references.
ISBN 978-0-9810433-2-6

1. Edward, Pauline, 1954-. 2. Course in miracles. 3. Spiritual life. 4. Spiritual biography. I. Title.

BP605.C68E38 2010   299'.93   C2010-905480-6

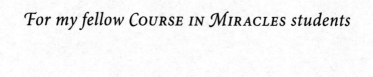

For my fellow COURSE IN MIRACLES students

CONTENTS

FOREWORD

WE HAD THE FORTUNE of meeting Pauline in Montreal while giving a workshop in 2007. We were impressed by her intelligence, as well as her eagerness to experience more of the teachings of *A Course in Miracles*, which we thought was impressive given the radical and sometimes controversial nature of the material. On top of that, she has a warmth about her and a clear understanding of this seemingly mysterious blue book called *A Course in Miracles*. The way she applies the teachings of the Course in her personal life, as discussed in this book, attests to her deep knowledge of the material and her willingness to do the work that the Course describes as a necessary part of the process of undoing what the Course calls the ego, the false, self-made concept of who we think we are. It does not surprise us that she is one of the teachers of God called forth to write on this subject, given her unique background as an astrologer-numerologist, Certified Professional Coach, and now speaker and author of several fine books, not to mention her interest at an early age in the works of some of the greatest spiritual teachers of our time, such as Thomas Merton, Ramana Maharshi and Paramahansa Yogananda.

My (Cindy's) own understanding of the Course deepened the more I actually applied the ideas in the workbook, which consists of 365 lessons, one for each day of the year. Being a student of the Course for six years, and Gary for eighteen, and now leading workshops around the world on this material, makes for a wonderful opportunity for us as a couple. It allows us to practise the principles and further ourselves along our chosen path to eventually achieve the kind of peace the Course talks about, the peace that is not of this world, the peace that leads to awakening from this seeming dream of separation.

We certainly appreciate Pauline's dedication and thorough examination of the Course, and also find her explanations and personal experiences very helpful. The undoing of the ego, uncovering the hidden unconscious guilt and bringing it to the light of truth, one of the goals of the Course, is not always a glamorous process. The clarity and spiritual insight Pauline brings to this work is a wonderful aid to furthering one's study of the Course and its teachings.

Leaving the Desert: Embracing the Simplicity of A Course in Miracles is one of the most practical spiritual books ever written. I (Gary) was struck by Pauline's ability to clearly and simply state the principles of the Course, from the beginning of her journey, through a genuine spiritual search, to her discovery of a new direction, to the understanding of miracles, and ultimately to the miracle of forgiveness in undoing the deviousness of the ego. I highly recommend this book to anyone who is on a spiritual path and especially to those who want to get on the fast track.

We know Pauline, and she lives these principles every day. We thank her for this wonderful book, and hope you will make the most of it!

Gary Renard
Best-selling author of *The Disappearance of the Universe*
and Cindy Lora-Renard
MA Spiritual Psychology
November 2010

ACKNOWLEDGMENTS

*A*LTHOUGH THIS BOOK IS very much the product of an intense personal journey of inner healing, it was also written in response to the many questions asked by clients, students and friends. I wish to express my deepest appreciation for the members of our Thursday evening *Course in Miracles* study group for their continued support and encouragement on this challenging journey. A special thanks to Mike Miller for his helpful suggestions, and also for his friendship. Of course, a huge heartfelt thank you to Veronica Schami for her expert editorial contribution. Thank you to Alexander Marchand for allowing me to use some of his cool illustrations in this edition.

There are no words that can adequately express the deep gratitude I will always feel for Dr. Kenneth Wapnick, founder of the Foundation for *A Course in Miracles*, for his unwavering devotion to the teachings of the Course. Without the help of his books and recordings, I can assure you that this journey would not have been made possible. Ken, I cannot thank you enough.

My deepest love and appreciation go to Helen Schucman and Bill Thetford, whose incredible dedication and courage allowed the transmission of this most significant of spiritual gifts, *A Course in Miracles*.

Thank you, all my brothers who asked for a better way, and of course, eternal gratitude for Jesus, who obliged.

REFERENCES

References to *A Course in Miracles* (ACIM) correspond to the numbering system of the Text (T), Workbook (W), Manual for Teachers (M) and Clarification of Terms (C) used in the Third Edition. For example:

T-27.VIII.6:2–5 corresponds to Text, Chapter 27, Section VIII, Paragraph 6, Sentences 2 to 5.

W-pI.132.5:1–3 corresponds to Workbook, Part I, Lesson 132, Paragraph 5, Sentences 1 to 3.

M-16.4:6 corresponds to Manual for Teachers, Question 16, Paragraph 4, Sentence 6.

C-3.4:1 corresponds to Clarification of Terms, Term 3, Paragraph 4, Sentence 1.

Our Love awaits us as we go to Him, and walks beside us showing us the way. He fails in nothing. He the End we seek, and He the Means by which we go to Him. (W-pII.302.2:1–3)

All for Nothing

Life is little more than an idle search
An endless series of futile attempts
To fill the emptiness
So long ago caused
by an insane decision
To give up All for nothing.

The price to pay
For a decision so crucial
Is a loss so profound
And a pain so excruciating
That its truth must be held
Behind a veil of forgetfulness.

Faint and fragile veiled remembrances
Of a peace and wholeness
Left far behind
Slip from my grasp
While I seek to replace
All with nothing.

So much time spent
Attending to hunger and need
To emptiness and loneliness
All the while keeping me
From seeing that in truth,
All remains as it always has been.

Pauline Edward
May 2009

Introduction

A STUDENT'S JOURNEY

> Simply do this: Be still, and lay aside all thoughts of what you are and what God is; all concepts you have learned about the world; all images you hold about yourself. Empty your mind of everything it thinks is either true or false, or good or bad, of every thought it judges worthy, and all the ideas of which it is ashamed. Hold onto nothing. Do not bring with you one thought the past has taught, nor one belief you ever learned before from anything. Forget this world, forget this course, and come with wholly empty hands unto your God. (W-pI.189.7:1–5)

From the Heart

THIS BOOK PICKS UP where *Making Peace with God* left off. It is the continuation of the journey that began when I adopted as my spiritual path the thought system of a phenomenal work called *A Course in Miracles*. It could have been subtitled "The Continuing Story of a Very Determined *Course in Miracles* Student," but then it might also have been called "The Continuing Story of a Very Resistant and Frightened *Course in Miracles* Student." Either would have been equally true. Anyone who has spent even just a few minutes reading the big book with the navy blue cover is likely to have concluded that *A Course in Miracles* is, at least at first glance, anything but simple. Those who know me also know that it was with tongue in cheek that I subtitled this work: "Embracing the Simplicity of *A Course in Miracles*." I am among those who found it extremely difficult to read; in fact, while I was pushing through a first reading, there were moments when I thought that I had become severely intellectually handicapped. Dyslexic, I thought I was.

As with *Making Peace with God*, this book was written in large part for my own healing. Writing is just something that I have always done. It helps me organize my thoughts and deepen my understanding and learning. Back in high school and college, I was an avid note-taker. Though for the most part I was not overly interested in learning the curriculum, if anything, note-taking kept me from falling asleep during class. At home, I would transcribe the notes into clean notebooks, adding illustrations and highlighting section titles with underlines and double underlines, maintaining one notebook for each subject, even algebra and geometry. In fact, my math notes were the neatest of all with colours and fancy shading for graphs and charts, algebraic equations cascading smoothly down the page. Clearly, I am a doer, not a thinker, and this book, in a way, is a collection of my *Course in Miracles* study notes. Another purpose for writing is to answer some of the questions asked by clients and fellow students of *A Course in Miracles*. Through their questions, comments and feedback, my own learning has grown.

Upon completing *Making Peace with God*, I honestly thought that I had written my last book. I wasn't sure why I was publishing in the first place, never for a moment considering myself an expert on the subject of spirituality, much less *A Course in Miracles*, but something from within guided me along the way. I would have been just as content to simply write in my journal with no ambitions for publication. As stated in *Making Peace with God*, I am an ordinary person, with perceptual abilities that are limited to the five physical senses. Other than occasional hunches, I have to work hard to sift through the noise in my mind in order to tune into inner guidance. I have never heard voices or seen spirits, nor have I been visited by beings from another time and place. This I take as a blessing of sorts, since, knowing myself all too well, such an experience would only have added to my already overly inflated sense of specialness, strengthening that little self that stands in the way of my true Self, making my journey home far longer than it need be.

Small blessings notwithstanding, it appears that whatever I need to learn will somehow always be brought to my attention. After the publication of *Making Peace with God*, although I was certain I had written my last book, the urge to write returned in full force. It was a compulsion I simply could not ignore. My journey with the Course was just beginning, a journey that by all appearances would require a thorough understanding of its fundamental message, what I suspected would no doubt be a very long journey. Though I had no illusions about my mastery of the teachings of *A Course in Miracles*, nor about my writing skills, I wavered between my love of writing and my niggling doubts. Occasionally, usually following a bout of self-doubt, something would happen to point me back in that direction. I would receive an email from a reader thanking me for having written my book, another would ask when the next one would be coming out, or someone would express how much they had related to my story. Many of my clients have expressed their interest in the Course, but at the same time they faced tremendous difficulty in understanding what it says. Very often, their questions came on the heels of my having written on the very same subject. Taking that as a message that I was to continue, back to writing I would go.

The most remarkable guidance came when I received an email from a channeller I had met only a couple of times. In the fall of 2008, Lisa LaJoie and I had shared a memorable conversation at a weekend conference at which, no doubt at the hand of fate, we had been assigned the same room. Lisa told me of how she had channelled messages from Jesus for one of her clients, an experience that had touched her deeply, and I shared my own story from *Making Peace with God*. From our common love of Jesus, a deep bond formed.

Lisa's email came early in the new year; it was a reply to an invitation to join my writers' group, but it was the unrelated postscript that caught my attention. "Did I mention your friend Holy J has a message for you? I think I mentioned it last year; I was told of it, I hope you have received it."

I replied that yes, she had mentioned a message, but that she had not passed it along. I think at the time I took her comment to be referring to the message of *A Course in Miracles*, that all I needed would be found within its pages, something I already knew. I never gave it further thought.

Lisa followed up with another email.

"I was hoping you got it some other way. I take those messages seriously. It was a sacred honour that he passed this on to me for you. People normally pay for my services to channel. I was surprised to get this message; I'm assuming it's because we bonded at the weekend and he really wants to get something across to you."

By then, I was totally confused, and so I responded that I wasn't sure what the message was, and that if he really wanted to get something across to me, I'd be happy to hear it, and could she please pass it along. To which she replied that, of course, we could make some time, but then when she finally understood my confusion, she sent another email explaining that she had trained herself to not pick up messages for others outside of consultation sessions, otherwise if she kept her channel open, she would receive messages all day long, from any source, for just anyone. She added that we had to be together, in person, in order for her to channel the message, from which point it was a straightforward matter of scheduling a meeting.

Never having experienced a reading with Lisa, I had no idea of what to expect, or even how the whole channelling process worked. I had always been somewhat wary of channelled material, since there was no way of verifying the source, and when Lisa sat across my desk for our unusual session, I must admit I felt a little apprehensive. We chatted casually for a few minutes and I relaxed a bit, but not completely. I would later learn that during our preliminary casual chat, Lisa was warming up, so to speak, preparing to tune in and receive the message, like booting up a computer and waiting for it to pick up a wireless connection. While Lisa tuned in, my anxiety grew. What if I were told that I was wasting my time and

4

shouldn't be doing the work I was doing? What if I were told to stop writing? Jesus had a message for *me*. It was difficult to work around the specialness that this one brief meeting might engender, so I decided to do my best to let things be, to not make a big deal of the fact that a channeller was about to give me a message from my all-time favourite spiritual teacher and healer. As best as I could, I emptied myself of all fears, expectations and thoughts of specialness; in silence I waited for my message.

Then it came. I wish I'd had the presence of mind to take notes; I had to remind myself to keep breathing. Although I do not recall the exact words of that first reading—there would be reminder readings later, just in case I forgot—I certainly recall its general meaning. To my great surprise, I was told that Jesus appreciated the work I was doing, for which he thanked me. He also said that I had walked with him before, long ago. Overwhelmed, it was all I could do to keep from crying the tears of longing, joy and profound relief that pushed their way up from the depths of my soul. Most of the message from that point was a blur. It was for me an extremely emotional experience, as it was for Lisa. To be in the presence of such pure love—there are simply no words to adequately describe the experience. Apparently, I was also told to write from the heart, but that bit of information was drowned out by my tears. Lisa would be urged to remind me of that part of the message months later during one of my moments of doubt. Afterwards, whenever I felt unsure about my writing, I would remember to write from the heart.

Journey into Truth

It was not so long ago that I doubted I would ever get through a complete reading of *A Course in Miracles*, having to literally force myself to string letters together to form words that made sense, as I tackled some of its more challenging sections. However, with continued dedication and, of course, my characteristic persistence, my perception of the teaching changed and my appreciation for its profound message grew tremendously. Despite my initial difficulties, to my great astonishment and delight, in time I came to acknowledge its simplicity. Although I doubt that I will ever fully appreciate the finer literary qualities of the text or that I will understand all of its psychological references, I did manage to reach a point where I could actually read it and have a fairly good idea of what it says. The next step, perhaps the most difficult of all, would be to figure out how to apply this extraordinary teaching. One thing was very clear, without direct application in my life, the message of the Course would have no significant impact on my spiritual well-being nor on any other aspect of my life; it would, in fact, remain little more than a fancy metaphysical teaching decorating the dark corners of my mind.

> You may complain that this course is not sufficiently specific for you to understand and use. Yet perhaps you have not done what it specifically advocates. This is not a course in the play of ideas, but in their practical application. (T-11.VIII.5:1–3)

To undertake the study of *A Course in Miracles* is truly to embark on a journey, and, like all journeys, it has its ups and its downs, its clear and easy stretches, but also its dark and lonely passages. When I first started to work with the Course, I felt lost as to how to apply its message in everyday situations. There was no doubt in my mind that I had finally found my path, that the Course's message was the truth, and that I would pursue it until my dying day, but it was a whole other matter to know what to do with it. As a practical, hands-on person with a brain that is more mechanically than academically inclined, I wanted to know what to do. If anything, I have always considered myself to be somewhat academically lazy, learning only as much as is required to get by or, perhaps more accurately, learning what is needed so I can do what I want to do. I have never studied simply for the sake of learning. In a way, this might have been a handicap of sorts, given my innate curiosity about complex issues such as why we are here or how the world came into existence in the first place, questions better addressed by the academically minded. But, in the end, curiosity and the profound desire to uncover the truth won over my lack of academic prowess. With persistence, I learned; actually, I learned way more than I had bargained for.

Practical Learning

Over the years, I came to understand that the best kind of knowledge is that which comes from direct, first-hand experience. Give me a concise how-to book or, better yet, show me how it's done, then I'll try it out for myself. This is how I have dealt with most of life's situations, big and small alike, from raising my daughters to learning astrology and numerology, working with computers, writing, publishing and running a business. With a little study, persistence and a lot of trial and error, I have always managed to figure things out for myself. That is, until *A Course in Miracles*. The book is, after all, a course—a concise, systematic and straightforward teaching program—and, as such, requires study. Yet, determined and persistent as I am, when it came to figuring out how to apply *A Course in Miracles* in my life, I hit a stone wall. Although the Course is a complete, highly individualized training system—perfect for a do-it-yourselfer such as myself—it wasn't long before I realized that its high level of sophistication would require a whole lot of study, persistence and trial and error. As I slowly began to discover its full depth and scope, I learned to accept that it would take many years of study before my practical mind could master the metaphysical and psychological principles essential to the effective application of its message on a day-to-day basis.

In my youth, I had been profoundly inspired by the stories of spiritual seekers, such as Thomas Merton's *The Seven Storey Mountain*, Yogananda's *Autobiography of a Yogi* and Arthur Osborne's *Ramana Maharshi and the Path of Self-Knowledge*. The more theoretical and academic books on spirituality left my practical mind cold, uninspired. My learning required a personal, human component. When I first began to study the Course, I was curious to know how other people had applied its message in their lives. But because *A Course in Miracles* was still very new, few people had as yet written about their own experiences. There were no "How to Live with ACIM" books, no real-life stories,[1] no tutorials and no manuals with step-by-step instructions on how to apply its teachings to everyday circumstances. So desperate was I for guidance, I think I would have settled for one of those cryptic IKEA assembly sheets. As one of my clients lamented, there were no *Coles Notes* to *A Course in Miracles*, only a huge book written in a highly sophisticated English, with a message that was designed to turn my entire belief system upside down or, more accurately, my upside-down thinking right side up.

Someone from our study group once asked who my teacher had been when I first began to study the Course. She wanted to know which study group I had belonged to, having herself been unable to find one nearby. "Jesus," I immediately replied, without giving her question a moment's thought. In answer to her puzzled look, I repeated that Jesus had been, and still was, my teacher. *A Course in Miracles* is his course and, to my mind, he is without a doubt its best teacher. Then I explained that I had listened to hundreds of hours of workshops by Course teacher Ken Wapnick, adding jokingly that Ken Wapnick was Jesus' TA par excellence.[2]

Over and above the theoretical understanding I gained from listening to these workshops, there was the added bonus of the more practical learning derived from the questions posed by participants. Workshop attendees brought up issues concerning those situations in their lives that presented problems and, like me, they wanted to know how to deal with them from the perspective of the Course. In listening to the answers given to their everyday concerns, my own understanding grew. In a way, these question-and-answer segments took the place of the real-life stories I would like to have read. Some

---

1. Other Course students have since written of their experiences. Visit my website for recommendations: www.PaulineEdward.com.
2. It was probably closer to 1000 hours at the time I was asked this question and 2000 at the time of this writing. A list of some of my favourite study aids can be found at the end of this book.

of these comments and observations have stayed with me for years, serving as lanterns, making the journey clearer and more certain.

In Search of the Happy Learner

My goal when I first became a student of *A Course in Miracles* was to get through a complete reading of the entire book, an exercise that I came to see as a rite of passage of sorts. When finished, though thoroughly pleased—and also, I must admit, very relieved—I declared, "Never again!" Although I knew that I would eventually read it again, it felt great to have gotten through it, even though I was well aware that I had not understood much of what I had read in the first place. But that was okay. Of one thing I was absolutely certain: *A Course in Miracles* provided the answers I had sought all my life and, most of all, in Jesus and the Holy Spirit, I had the best teachers in the world. Having found what I had been looking for, I wasn't about to quit anytime soon. What remained was to learn how to use it. That would be the hard part.

> This course requires almost nothing of you. It is impossible to imagine one that asks so little, or could offer more. (T-20. VII.1:7–8)

Before long, I came to understand that *A Course in Miracles* was brilliantly conceived to take its students on a profound journey of complete and total personal transformation and healing. Though what it asks of its students is deceptively simple, its power and effectiveness should not be underestimated. Though I never expected it to be easy, being of an intrinsically impatient temperament, I wanted the entire process to move along as quickly and, naturally, as painlessly as possible. I continued my daily ritual of listening to Ken Wapnick workshops and started to reread the Course. As instructed, I opened my eyes and looked harder and deeper at what was going on in my mind, increasingly vigilant for my thoughts, motivations, desires, intentions and reactions. Gradually, I became better acquainted with the thought system with which I completely identified—the wrong-minded thought system of the ego.

The Holy Spirit needs a happy learner, in whom His mission can be happily accomplished. You who are steadfastly devoted to misery must first recognize that you are miserable and not happy. The Holy Spirit cannot teach without this contrast, for you believe that misery is happiness. (T-14.II.1:1–3)

As I worked more and more with the Course, my understanding of its message grew, but, to my profound dismay, instead of growing happier and more peaceful, I began to grow distraught with my life. I lost interest in most things that had previously provided the motivation I needed to accomplish the many things I believed to be important. A cloud of futility fell over me while aspects of myself that I frankly found distasteful were uncovered. Deeply buried emotions, such as anger, resentment, intolerance, blame, guilt and, worst of all, hatred, rose to the surface. The "nice" person I had been all my life began to fade while I became a miserable, grumpy and unhappy learner.

But still, I didn't quit, and as I continued to scratch beneath the surface, the false veneer of civility I had cultivated over the years began to grow dangerously thin. As might be expected, my incessant delving into the dark corners of my mind inevitably stirred up fear and deep resistance. Although a part of me was clearly enthusiastic about my spiritual excavation job, another part was far less thrilled, expressing its resistance with a variety of persistent and debilitating aches and pains in my back, shoulders and arms. After having laid out the outline and structure for this book, I lost the use of my right arm entirely; damage to the left arm wasn't far behind. Unable to spend more than a few minutes at the computer, my work on this book, an essential ingredient to my healing process, ground to a halt.

Not wanting to remain in this dark phase of my journey any longer than necessary, I relaxed my efforts, making it my next goal to become a happy learner. Being a miserable, suffering, unhappy learner wasn't much fun, although, from the ego's perspective, it did have its perks, principally the reinforcement of my separateness through identification with my body and my feelings of desolation.

I felt pain, therefore, I must exist as an individual, separate from my source. However, not being a big fan of pain in any of its various forms, I rededicated myself to a closer study of the message of the Course. Clearly, there was nowhere else to turn; certainly not to my old beliefs. So it was that my daily prayer to the Holy Spirit became, "Please teach me to become a happy learner."

> If you would be a happy learner, you must give everything you have learned to the Holy Spirit, to be unlearned for you. And then begin to learn the joyous lessons that come quickly on the firm foundation that truth is true. For what is builded there *is* true, and built on truth. The universe of learning will open up before you in all its gracious simplicity. With truth before you, you will not look back. (T-14.II.6:1–5)

Applying what bits and pieces of learning I was gathering from the Course, I was able to use the dark shadows of my experiences as my classroom, a necessary step in my healing process. Ultimately, I knew that I would never be at peace until I had, through the Course's unique process of forgiveness, completely removed the blockages to Love's presence, a goal that would take a little while—okay, a very long while—but I was equal to the task. In the end, I came to the conclusion that the quickest and simplest way to experience the peace of God, which is the goal set forth by *A Course in Miracles* for its students, is to do what Jesus says. Jesus answered our collective plea for another way of dealing with life and the world in the form of this remarkable work. It is his promise that if we follow these teachings, we will feel better and, ultimately, experience peace. If that isn't motivation enough, he also tells us that the practice of the Course will save time, not only for myself, but also for whoever is the recipient of my forgiveness practice. That, in itself, is the perfect carrot to dangle in front of an intrinsically impatient temperament such as mine.

> The miracle minimizes the need for time.... The miracle substitutes for learning that might have taken thousands

of years…. The miracle shortens time by collapsing it, thus eliminating certain intervals within it. (T-1.II.6:1, 7, 9)

The aim of this book is to share my personal exploration of some of the basic principles of *A Course in Miracles*, along with the practical ways in which I learned to apply its message. Every person will take from the Course what they need at this time in their life. While many have taken bits and pieces of this teaching and adapted it for their own learning needs, in order to simplify matters for myself, I have accepted it wholly, as it is, without reservation or compromise. Although this approach may seem to require a lot of effort and diligent application—and, believe me, there is no doubt that it does, at least at first—in the end, it certainly makes the process simpler. All that is asked of its students is to follow the training program as instructed: study the text, practise the lessons and look with the vision of the Holy Spirit. Because this is the approach I have adopted, it does not follow that it is the only one; it is simply the one that works for me. Each student will be guided to find his or her own way of approaching and applying the teachings of *A Course in Miracles*.

Though the Course does not use many complicated words or terms, its sentence structure is at times complex, as are some of its psychological references, requiring very careful reading. I am absolutely certain though, that for those who express an earnest desire to learn this thought system, guidance will come. It is also not necessary to spend hundreds of hours attempting to understand every line of the text. It appears complicated and complex because we perceive ourselves, and our world, as complicated and complex. In truth, its message is extremely simple. With time and diligent study and, more importantly, a little willingness and a whole lot of practice, understanding follows.

For many people, when they first start studying the Text of the Course they think it may as well be written in a foreign language. This is because J presents the Course *as if* you already understand what he's talking about, even though he knows that on the level of form you do not understand a lot of it. Ideas are introduced, dropped, and then taught again later in more detail. The thought system builds upon itself in order for you to learn it. The learning of the Course must be seen as a process, not an event.[3]

Though *A Course in Miracles* speaks to us where we believe ourselves to be, it is designed to bring us to an experience of who we truly are, as God created us. It was given to us from a place of complete love, and so its message contains only love. For the sincere seeker, all that is needed is to be still a while and listen; your memory of the truth of who you are will lead the way. The best approach for working with this spiritual path is patient, gentle dedication. To journey with *A Course in Miracles* is to engage in a lifelong process of removing the barriers to the truth.

Since there were no Thomas Mertons or Yoganandas of *A Course in Miracles*, I had to figure out how to integrate its teachings into my life pretty much by myself. In the process, I encountered the darkest recesses of my mind, but I also experienced glimpses of joy and peace that reach beyond anything that is of this world. While, for the most part, I travelled this road on my own, I never felt completely alone: Jesus and the Holy Spirit were, and are, always by my side, helping me with this process. This is very much the story of one student, muddling along, learning to apply the message of *A Course in Miracles* in her life and yes, it is written from the heart.

Can you imagine what a state of mind without illusions is? How it would feel? Try to remember when there was a time,—perhaps a minute, maybe even less—when nothing came to interrupt your peace; when you were certain you were loved and safe. Then try to picture what it would be like to have that moment be extended to the end of time and to eternity. Then let the sense of quiet that you felt be multiplied a hundred times, and then be multiplied another hundred more. (W-107.2:1–5)

---

3. Gary Renard, *The Disappearance of the Universe*, page 105.

Chapter 1

IN SEARCH OF TRUE SPIRITUALITY

No one can fail who seeks to reach the truth.

Be glad that search you must. Be glad as well to learn you
search for Heaven, and must find the goal you really want.
No one can fail to want this goal and reach it in the end.
(W-pI.131.4:1–3)

The Spirituality of the New Millennium

*T*HERE IS NO DENYING that, at the start of the new millen-
nium, the spiritual quest, in its various forms, ancient and contemporary, has truly come alive. The spiritualities and philosophies
of the day vary as much in style as they do in content, covering, it
seems, the full spectrum of the human experience from the desire
for a better life in the world to the search for the truth about the
origins of life and the meaning of existence. We want to be happy.
We want healing. We want peace. We want to love and be loved. We
want forgiveness. We want a sense of fulfillment and accomplishment. We want the abundance to which we feel entitled. We want
to feel safe. We want to create a better world for ourselves, for our
children and for our children's children. We want to know that our
life has had meaning and that we have made a difference.

There are many reasons for the growth of this trend, one being
the common practice of calling on the Divine in times of economic,
social or political uncertainty. The world in which we live is certainly fast-paced and in a constant state of change for most people,

but also in a state of war, suffering and strife for far too many. When under severe stress or in the grip of traumatic circumstances, we tend to turn toward God, religion or spiritual mentors. Confused, frightened and unable to make sense of a world that seems to have gone insane, we look beyond ourselves to higher wisdom in search of answers, needing clarity and understanding, and, especially, seeking reassurance and hope.

Another factor contributing to the rise in popularity of spirituality, at least in the Western world, is the rapid growth of the aging population. The fact that we live longer today than ever before means that we are exposed to more life experiences, both good and bad. Sooner or later, after having gone around the block a few times, chances are that we will wonder, if not about the origins of life, then at least about what lies beyond. As the end approaches and the inevitability of death casts its shadow on our life's journey, we want to know more about the mysteries of life and death. What will happen when I die? Is there life after death or do we only have one chance? Will I be remembered or forgotten? Will I reconnect with loved ones or will I be forever alone? Will I be forgiven for my mistakes or will I be judged and condemned to atone for my sins? Is there a God? Is there a Heaven? Is there a divine purpose for my existence? Much of this questioning is motivated by the fear of the unknown, in particular, the fear of death.

To alleviate these feelings of uncertainty, many will search for a teaching that will provide them with the reassurance that everything will be all right when they die, that in the end, their life has not been for nothing. Some will find comfort in the promises made by traditional religions, and as their life's journey comes to a close, they will turn toward their childhood faith. Ultimately, we seek reassurance that our existence has served a purpose. God, or a fair and just greater power, will see to it that we will be forgiven for our faults and blessed for our efforts, no matter how feeble they may have been. After we are gone, our loved ones will cling to the memories of our time together; our brief existence in the world will extend a while longer. After the passing of a couple of generations, those memories, too, will fade.

The explosion of the Internet and the extraordinarily rapid advancement of communication technologies over the past thirty years may be the biggest single factor contributing to this growth. International and interfaith boundaries are disappearing completely, while information proliferates and spreads quicker than wildfire. The electronic web abounds with an ever-growing abundance of information, products and services dedicated to spirituality and personal growth, promising hope of a better world, enlightenment, happiness, awakening and a direct and personal connection with the Divine.

In recent years, the self-help, alternative health, self-development and varied life skills industries have merged almost seamlessly into the increasingly noisy and chaotic mainstream marketplace, attracting young and old alike. This trend is indicative not only of the very real need in our time for answers to cries for help, but also of an openness to exploring broader and deeper facets of the human experience. Bookstore shelves, virtual and traditional, are overflowing with thousands of titles promising to deliver abundance, joy, wealth, love, peace, healing and success, many of which have proven to be beneficial for thousands of people seeking solace from the pain, suffering, stress, worries and anxieties of life in an uncertain, ever-changing and increasingly challenging world. Yet, despite all the calls for help and the many obliging responses, turmoil, starvation, suffering, illness, war and conflict have yet to be replaced by peace, love, kindness and a sense of the oneness of humanity. In fact, our distresses and challenges are probably growing as rapidly as are our supposed advancements.

The Desecration of Spirituality

In my consulting practice, as well as through my social and business networks, I regularly meet people who would describe themselves as being, if not on a specific spiritual path, at the very least, spiritually inclined. However, to my understanding, much of what passes for spirituality today is actually self-help or, perhaps more generally, life skills. Many of the self-help approaches of the day find their roots in works that date back, in some cases, nearly two centuries to the New Thought Movement. These include works by doctors, writers, lecturers and authors such as Orison Swett Marden (b. 1850), Samuel Smiles (b. 1812), Dr. Joseph Murphy (b. 1898, *The Power of Your Subconscious Mind*), Maxwell Maltz (b.1899, *Psychocybernetics*), Norman Vincent Peale (b. 1898, *The Power of Positive Thinking*), Dale Carnegie (b. 1888), Napoleon Hill (b. 1883) and Wallace Wattles (b. 1860, *The Science of Getting Rich*).

As many of these authors were themselves influenced by the religious views of their time, it is not unusual to find related undertones reflected in their teachings. In these works, as well as in those of many of today's popular teachers, it is common practice to associate God's will with our good fortune, joy and well-being. Since, as many religions claim, we are created by God and God is perfect, eternal and therefore not lacking anything, it naturally follows that He must will for us nothing less than perfect abundance, health, prosperity, peace and happiness. As His creations, it is our right to participate in His infinite abundance. It seems logical to conclude that our well-being is in accordance with the Divine will, while unhappiness, scarcity, misery, loneliness, illness and, in fact, suffering of any kind are not part of our natural inheritance.

We are told that by placing our faith in God, the source of unlimited abundance, all that we desire will be ours. If we are not experiencing a life of abundance, joy and peace, it is surely because our faith is lacking. If our faith is lacking, then a simple modification to our thinking patterns will correct our error. Our thoughts determine the life we live. By changing our thoughts we are told that we will change our lives and, by extension, the world. Once faith has been engaged, a life of happiness, abundance and joy is sure to follow. Does this mean that those who live in comfort and experience good fortune are being rewarded for their good faith? And what of those who were not raised to know or even think of

God? Are they destined for a life of suffering and scarcity? There are plenty of fortunate individuals who do not believe in much other than the mighty dollar, and many more sincere believers who live in abject poverty.

With or without a belief in God, each person will address the question of the meaning of life by adopting a philosophy or belief system that works with his or her unique personality style. Given that these are the glory days of the information age, it seems that there is a suitable thought system for each temperament somewhere out there. Many believe that we are heading into an enlightened age, citing this growing interest in spirituality as proof. Some think that an enlightened era will somehow magically swoop down on earth at an appointed time, bringing peace and abundance for a select few, or even for all. Yet, no one asks *who* might send this wave of enlightenment on earth, or why now and not at some other time in history. Why not during World War II or the Rwandan genocide, or any one of the many shameful moments that darken the history of humanity?

Then there are those kind, gentle souls, genuinely concerned with the welfare of others, always ready, and often very much involved in helping others. They have faith in a God that is just and kind. They earnestly believe that by practising kindness, the world will change, one kind, loving act at a time. Though well-meaning and to a limited extent beneficial, this philosophy of life is somewhat like attempting to put out a forest fire with a thimbleful of water. It can be rewarding to know that you are doing something to help, no matter how seemingly insignificant, but you cannot put out a fire as long as fuel continues to be poured onto it. Likewise, how can the woes of the world be healed unless their cause is first identified?

Others look upon the universe as being in a marvellous evolutionary process of unfolding. They believe that this unfolding is a way for God to manifest Himself so that He can know Himself. Furthermore, since God is in all of us, we are all part of this Divine expression. Yet again, this begs the question, if God is all knowing, why does He have to get to know Himself? Doesn't He know that there are millions of people who suffer here on earth?

Another line of thinking centres on the belief that our suffering is given to us by God, that for reasons known only to Him, He has given us lessons to learn. We are told that we should learn our lessons gladly and be grateful for the small blessings with which we have been graced. In our struggles, we will know our perfection. All is unfolding according to the Divine Plan. We are encouraged to rely on our faith to support us through our times of suffering and difficulty and, in the end, we will be rewarded with the keys to the Kingdom of Heaven. Again, one must ask, how could a God of perfect love assign to His children lessons that involve even the faintest aspect of suffering, pain and loss of any kind? Why would He not just give the keys to His children? Also, if God is perfect, then what He creates must also be perfect, in His image and likeness. What He creates does not need to unfold, learn, grow or develop.

There is the increasingly popular "it's all good" philosophy of life, its adherents blithely brushing off bad things, focusing instead on the positive. Though a cute tag line for a marketing campaign, this amounts to little more than a philosophy of convenient denial. Its disciples decide to see only what is good, no matter how bad a situation might be, choosing to leave matters in the hands of a wise and all-knowing universal principle or God. They believe that their faith in this higher, benevolent power, combined with a positive outlook will protect them from harm and ensure prolonged happiness. This powerful combination of faith and attitude allows them to ride the tides of their lives relatively unscathed. "Life's good," they say, and with reason. They have set it up, at least for the most part, to have the appearance of being good. The premise behind this line of thinking being that if you nurture nice thoughts, you are apt to attract a nice life, which works for a while, at least until things stop going the way you want them to. Then there is the problem of lack of universality. It may be good for you, but, like most of these New Age outlooks, it certainly isn't good for the millions of people on the planet who are ill, starving or experiencing some form of conflict or hardship.

Taking a closer look at some of the popular beliefs that centre on the mastery of thought, intention and the harnessing of the power of mind, here, too, we find glaring discrepancies in the logic. If it were true that we can change the future, even create the future we desire by the power of our thoughts and intentions, then it must also be true that we have created the world in which we now live with our past thoughts and intentions. That being the case, why then did we "create" a world of struggle, danger, hardship, competition and inevitable death? Why did we make bodies with never-ending needs? If we are really "co-creators with God," as many believe us to be, then why did we not create a world that shares in His perfection?

This remains a limited view of the power of mind. It does not address the cause of the "not so nice" things that happen in a life, even if occasional, or apparently accidental. Nor does it address the nasty things going on elsewhere in the world or even in our own backyards. Are innocent children who are maimed or killed by stray bullets being punished for their "not so nice" thoughts? Is a child born deformed and in pain paying for his inability to adequately manage his thoughts? This view of the power of the mind only works if it is not applied universally. If it is not universally applicable, then it cannot be true, for truth must be universal.

A woman sitting next to me at a networking breakfast was discussing the importance of a positive body image. She was in the business of helping people lose weight and feel good about themselves with her cleansing and weight loss products. She explained how she had come to realize that since God created, and no doubt loved her body, it would be rude of her to not love it back. Though a cute Unique Selling Proposition, the problem with this kind of thinking is that it is, once again, not logical. Why would a God of infinite goodness, fairness and wisdom create one body that is healthy and another that is ridden with disease and imperfection? How could He create even one deformed body?

Another woman at the same event marvelled at the power of intention. She had wished for one of the door prizes and won it. "It's true, the power of intention really works," she said to me, clearly pleased to have mastered the law of attraction. Although inspiring for some, this amounts to little more than magical thinking—mind tricks for the mundane. The ability to associate thought with the material, though fun and perhaps an entertaining distraction, is not a spiritual act. Will this person express the same marvel when she falls ill with the flu? Then she would probably say that a flu virus made her ill, not her thoughts. But then who put the flu virus out there? Actually, who put "out there" out there?

Life in the Desert

In *Making Peace with God*, I likened the practice of tapping into the power of the mind to accomplish specific goals such as acquiring a new house, attracting a loving relationship, securing a better job or attracting wealth somewhat like being in the middle of the desert with a handful of dried beans and learning that by aligning will with the natural power of mind, you can magically manifest a bucket of fresh water. Excitedly, you plant your seeds, add a little water and before you know it, you have healthy seedlings growing at your feet. Encouraged by your success, you use the fledgling power of your mind to manifest a little creek, and now you have enough water to nurse your plants to maturity. With practice, your mind grows to be so powerful that you are able to manifest a flowing river and soon your garden has blossomed into a flourishing oasis. Now you are able to feed your family and friends, which all seems great, except that no matter how great the power of your mind, no matter how abundant your oasis and how many mouths you feed, the fact remains that you are still in the desert. As Jesus told Helen Schucman, the scribe of *A Course in Miracles*,

> A desert is a desert is a desert. You can do anything you want in it, but you *cannot* change it from what it *is*. It still lacks

water. This is why it *is* a desert. The thing to do with a desert is to *leave*.[1]

For many people, in fact probably for most, at least in the West, the pursuit of worldly accomplishments and the triumph over the everyday battles presented by the normal challenges of life in a body in this world will keep them sufficiently busy and satisfied so that they will never really feel the call to question the meaning of existence. Many of the people I know fall into this category, being generally content with their lives and not particularly inclined, or otherwise motivated, to pursue the matter any further than necessary. If the oasis is thriving, if emotional and material needs are being met, then why question the nature and origins of the desert? It's all good!

While learning to attract abundance, love and success in your life, even if only to make enough money to feed your family, may certainly be an invaluable skill to acquire, it is far from what can be called spiritual. These are life skills. Although such practices involve the development of the mind and, to a certain extent, faith in the process, the goal is the satisfaction of material rather than spiritual needs. There appears to be some confusion between the search for a happier and more abundant life in the world and what can appropriately be considered the quest for spiritual fulfillment.

Putting Spirit Back into Spirituality

Essentially, spirit is not about this world, nor is it even *of* this world. To not address this point might result in an incomplete experience, especially for the sincere seeker of truth. The *Canadian Oxford Dictionary* defines spirit as "the intelligent non-physical part of a person" and spiritual as "of or relating to the human spirit or soul; not of physical things; concerned with sacred or religious things; holy; divine; inspired." Clearly, what is of spirit pertains to that which is non-material. Has spirit been reduced to a vague pop concept to be dropped into conversations as a show of sophisticated

---

1. Kenneth Wapnick, Ph.D., *Absence from Felicity*, page 236.

broad-mindedness? If we put spirit back into spirituality, what would the spiritual quest resemble in an era of unprecedented technological and material advancement and abundance? Can the sincere seeker shake off the noise and distractions of the world long enough to search for and hear the truth in the quiet of the mind?

The principle of God, the Divine, Supreme Being or Primal Source, which can hardly be ignored when discussing spirituality, is addressed in thousands of different ways by the religions and spiritualities of the world. Our sacred texts, holy books and mythologies are filled with references to God's involvement with the world and with mankind. God created the heavens and the earth, the first man and the first woman. He sends plagues to punish the wicked and protects the virtuous from His wrath. He condemns the sinner and promises rewards for the righteous. We pray for His mercy in times of crisis, and thank Him for our good fortune when we get what we want. We say, "It's God's will that I attracted this happy circumstance into my life." Even in the most trying times, we believe there is a higher purpose behind our suffering. "It's all part of the greater plan," we say, with simplistic and naive resignation.

For those who stop and really think about it, this kind of reasoning quickly becomes illogical, leaving behind an awkward trail of additional unanswered questions. How could a loving God, our Father, favour one of His children over another? How could He give one person a Mercedes while there remains even one person on earth who will have nothing to eat today? What kind of God would be so insensitive and so biased? Thanking God for material abundance or attributing a higher purpose to suffering may be self-serving and naive, but it is not spiritual.

In most religions and spiritualities, God, or the Source, is defined as being perfect, eternal, whole and infinite. If this world was indeed created by such a God, again, the starting point for most spiritual thought systems, then what He created must also be perfect. Yet it doesn't take an enlightened mind to see that this world is far from being perfect. Some troubling questions remain: How could God create a world that is imperfect? How could God create anything that is even the slightest bit less than perfect? There can be only one logical answer to these questions: God did *not* create this world. In fact, He could not have created this world, otherwise He would not be perfect, for what He creates must be like Himself. This line of questioning leaves us in a rather disturbing situation. If God did not create this world, then who did?

While most people will be content to live in an oasis of their own making, or even just a reasonably acceptable facsimile thereof, for a few, the oasis has lost its charm and the desert looms large, lifeless and unappealing. These souls hunger for a different truth, seeing that there is far too much that is wrong with this world, a place that, by all appearances, has been abandoned by God. They wonder if there is something other than the desert, which they have begun to see as a place of desolation and inevitable death. Tired of the suffering and the struggles of life in a body in a seemingly godless world, they embark on a quest for answers to the age-old questions concerning the meaning of existence.

One of the first stops for the spiritual novice is the Internet, the information Mecca of the day. There, the seeker is most definitely very well served. A person can spend a lifetime exploring and experimenting with the thousands of different techniques and thought systems available, a pursuit that many will embrace with great gusto and enthusiasm. Sometimes, even when adequate answers are not found, the journey itself will bring a sense of purpose to the life. At least I am actively searching; I am doing something. A feeling of belonging can also be experienced when other seekers are encountered along the way, providing an opportunity for sharing that can temporarily fill the inner void. It is comforting to realize that we are not alone in our quest.

Sorting through this abundance of information can be not only time consuming, but for those who are just beginning the journey, to a certain extent, confusing and sometimes even overwhelming. Many people will sip at the fountains of the various spiritual and metaphysical teachings, never fully mastering any one in particular. Some will take bits and pieces from different schools of thought in search of those teachings that validate their beliefs and suit their personality style, but not having adequately questioned their original beliefs, these bits and pieces can only add to the confusion.

True Holiness

Every day, thousands of emails bearing messages of hope and wisdom from our spiritual teachers flow through the World Wide Web, just waiting to be picked up and taken seriously by those who are ready to hear them. Who has not been brought to tears by simple stories of loving kindness and forgiveness, tales that resonate with a long-buried memory of something wonderful and beautiful that lies deep within us. The words of our favourite teachers— Jesus, Buddha, Ramana, Rumi and so many others—act as beacons, reaching out and calling to us from beyond the far reaches of the desert, seemingly so far, far away. Then, before we know it, the busyness of the day quickly rushes in and what might have been a moment's brush with truth quickly dissipates, folding itself once again into memory, to be stirred up again when the next gem is caught in the daily net.

True spirituality, as reflected in the ancient teachings of India and the Orient, for example, is almost a foreign concept in Western culture, which is clearly more concerned with the world of form and matter than it is with detachment and the illusory nature of the cosmos. If true spirituality is concerned with spirit, then true holiness appears to be absent in most so-called spiritualities today. The truly holy are generally simple, quiet people, motivated by non-material goals, their hearts set on the desire to know God. In his conversations with M. Beaufort, one such holy man, Brother Lawrence, related

> ... that God had done him a singular favor, in his conversion at the age of eighteen.
> That in the winter, seeing a tree stripped of its leaves, and considering that within a little time the leaves would be renewed and after that the flowers and fruit appear, he received a high view of the Providence and Power of God, which has never

since been effaced from his soul. That this view had perfectly set him loose from the world, and kindled in him such a love of God, that he could not tell whether it had increased during the more than forty years he had lived since.[2]

The truly holy do not see themselves as special, nor do they seek to develop special powers of mind or of any kind. They place no value in the things of the world; they are, in fact, *in* this world, but not *of* this world. They live and breathe devotion, simplicity and humility. They place their entire trust in God, and their actions are devoid of ego motivations. Their will is His will, and this is their only true joy. Life in the world, in a body, is simply an interlude, a quiet inconvenience to be borne out until the day they rejoin their Father in Heaven. Such is the stuff of the truly holy soul.

A Spirituality for the Western Mind

For those long-time seekers who were not born holy, yet who have a yearning for truth and for peace of a lasting kind, a longing for that place that is our true home, the answers provided by most contemporary spiritualities, as well as the teachings of the traditional religions, will eventually be found to be lacking. This is particularly the case for Westerners, whose cultures are far removed from those that gave birth to the ancient spiritual traditions of the world, and for whom it almost seems as though material success has been elevated to the ranks of spiritual attainment. Those who seek for answers in the traditional philosophies and spiritualities of the Orient are faced with outdated mythologies and symbolism that is difficult to understand, and nearly impossible to apply in everyday life. Short of donning long orange robes and open sandals and abandoning the condo for a Himalayan cave, the contemporary spiritual student appears to have few options.

The roads this world can offer seem to be quite large in number, but the time must come when everyone begins to see how like

---

2. Brother Lawrence, *The Practice of the Presence of God and the Spiritual Maxims*, page 5.

they are to one another. Men have died on seeing this, because they saw no way except the pathways offered by the world. And learning they led nowhere, lost their hope. And yet this was the time they could have learned their greatest lesson. All must reach this point, and go beyond it. (T-31.IV.3:3–7)

Some seekers have simply given up; they've been around the block a few too many times and have seen that nothing really changes, a conclusion that is often accompanied by profound feelings of disillusionment, loneliness and even hopelessness. They would like to believe that there must be something other than what their experience has shown, something that makes more sense than what they have been taught, some other way of looking at life and the world, but they don't know where to turn. It is upon having reached this dark place in their pursuit of the truth that many seekers have been introduced to the radical new spiritual thought system of *A Course in Miracles*.

Many people who have been on the spiritual path for a while will have heard of *A Course in Miracles*. Popular writers and speakers such as Wayne Dyer, Eckhart Tolle and Marianne Williamson quote from it for inspiration and teaching purposes. What makes the Course unique is that it addresses certain fundamental issues that most other spiritual thought systems do not, such as the problem of the imperfection of a world created by a perfect God; the suffering of God's children; and the true purpose of life in a body in the world. It does this in a form that is suited for the Western seeker, using language and imagery with which we can relate, while respecting the pace, obligations and generally frenetic nature of our contemporary lifestyles.

Above all, *A Course in Miracles* provides the sincere seeker with the guidance needed for leaving the oasis in the desert and attaining that elusive place of perfect peace for which we all so deeply yearn. In fact, it provides a vehicle for traversing the seemingly impossible divide between our false selves as bodies and our true Selves as Spirit, as God created us. The following chapters will serve to explore some of the principles that make *A Course in Miracles* unique, along with some of the common challenges faced by many of its students, not the least by this author.

> Tolerance for pain may be high, but it is not without limit. Eventually everyone begins to recognize, however dimly, that there *must* be a better way. As this recognition becomes more firmly established, it becomes a turning point. (T-2.III.3:5–7)

Chapter 2

A BOLD NEW SPIRITUALITY

Do not be concerned about how you can learn a lesson so completely different from everything that you have taught yourself. How would you know? Your part is very simple. You need only recognize that everything you learned you do not want. Ask to be taught, and do not use your experiences to confirm what you have learned. When your peace is threatened or disturbed in any way, say to yourself:

I do not know what anything, including this, means. And so I do not know how to respond to it. And I will not use my own past learning as the light to guide me now. (T-14.XI.6:1–9)

A Path for the Long-time Seeker

THOSE WHO COME TO *A Course in Miracles* usually have previously been engaged in some form of pursuit of truth and healing; a few have been so engaged for a very long time, if not an entire lifetime. For some, it is the Course that somehow found *them*. As the saying goes, when the student is ready, the teacher will come, and in many cases, the teacher comes in the shape of a big blue book. A few will instantly know that this is the path for them, especially those disheartened seekers who have all but given up the search for truth. Many will obtain a copy of the book, only to glance at its contents, attempt to read the first few chapters, perhaps skip ahead in search of more readable content, then set it aside with the intention of returning to it "one day." While many people will give, or have given, it a try, perhaps most will not give it the time and effort that is needed to experience the full benefits that might be gained with a complete and proper study. At first glance, for many, if not most, people, *A Course in Miracles* simply seems far too difficult!

> The escape from darkness involves two stages: First, the recognition that darkness cannot hide. This step usually entails fear. Second, the recognition that there is nothing you want to hide even if you could. This step brings escape from fear. When you have become willing to hide nothing, you will not only be willing to enter into communion but will also understand peace and joy. (T-1.IV.1:1–5)

Many beginner students of the Course feel that what it says somehow makes sense, but then when they try to understand it and apply its message in their lives, they hit a wall. As a spiritual thought system, it is refreshingly logical and surprisingly straightforward, but it is also unequivocal in its message. It says what it says without compromise. Furthermore, the full breadth of the message of the Course is usually not grasped until years of study have been undertaken. This is not because its students are intellectually deficient or because it is impossible to read. Rather, this occurs because of our profound resistance to accepting what it says.

For the true seeker, *A Course in Miracles* is likely to lead to the undoing of a deeply engrained perception of the self, a perception that the Course says is false. It asks that we be willing to look honestly at this self with which we are so intimately bound and identified, this special, unique and distinct individual, something most of us have worked very hard at developing throughout our lives, this self that we so deeply cherish. It takes its students on a journey of profound and total self-excavation. And though at times frightening, and perhaps even terrifying, it is a journey that leads to rewards far beyond anything this world will ever offer, the gifts of true vision, wholeness and the lasting peace of God.

In my consulting work as an astrologer-numerologist, clients frequently ask me to explain exactly what is *A Course in Miracles.*

Usually, those asking the question have attempted to read it at least once. A typical comment is "I tried to read it, but I found it too difficult to understand," a remark that is often accompanied by a look of bafflement, even surprise. My clients are generally intelligent, and many are well-read and highly educated. To have difficulty reading a book that was featured on *Oprah* can be somewhat disconcerting, if not outright embarrassing. When I first began to study the Course, I did not feel confident enough with the material to give a simple, clear answer to those who asked about it. I would simply refer them to *The Disappearance of the Universe* by Gary Renard. Since this is the work that opened the door for me, I would explain, it might be helpful for them too. It is a wonderfully straightforward and comprehensive introduction to the Course, far more than I could hope to offer on my own.

Gradually, I grew more comfortable with the teaching and eventually began to formulate my own responses, knowing full well, however, that a brief answer could never fully do it justice. Now, whenever asked about the Course, I give it up to the Holy Spirit, confident that He will help me answer the question at the level that will be most helpful. I understand that when speaking about this teaching, I am addressing a part of the mind that remembers the truth, so that, even though the person may appear to not fully understand my words, what I say will be heard at the level at which the truth can be recognized. Since minds are joined, the questions of other students are also my questions, and so my own understanding grows. As I proceed with my response, I smile as I catch a look of confusion blended with a spark of hope. I understand that the confusion stems from the part of the mind that has been trained to believe that what is false is true and what is true is false, while the light of hope comes from that part of the mind we all share, the part that remembers the truth. This chapter is an expanded version, with variations, of my answer to the question, "What is *A Course in Miracles?*"

The Holy Spirit, seeing where you are but knowing you are elsewhere, begins His lesson in simplicity with the fundamental teaching that truth is true. This is the hardest lesson you will ever learn, and in the end the only one. Simplicity is very difficult for twisted minds. Consider all the distortions you have made of nothing; all the strange forms and feelings and actions and reactions that you have woven out of it. Nothing is so alien to you as the simple truth, and nothing are you less inclined to listen to. (T-14.II.2:1–5)

Warning Label

For those who are uncertain as to whether or not *A Course in Miracles* is the path for them, an introductory overview of what it is, what it says and what it requires of its students may be helpful. I have met many people who have stood on the fence, intrigued enough, but not knowing how to approach the Course. Because some of its principal teachings are so fundamentally contrary to what most of us have been taught and have accepted without question as truth for most of our lives, easing into the subject may help prevent some of the common errors and misinterpretations experienced by beginning students. Without a proper frame of reference, it is easy to misconstrue the message entirely, and almost impossible to do the work that will ensure the attainment of its goal of peace.

Recalling my initial reaction—rather, my initial shock—when I first started to study *A Course in Miracles*, I can't help but think that perhaps it should come with a warning label. From the very first page, it dives into the heart of the matter without preamble, without preparation, leaving the reader reeling with a mixture of bafflement and a faint spark of recognition, but, usually, with nowhere to turn for help. A first reading of *A Course in Miracles* is much like trying to hitch a ride on a moving train. You must really want to go where that train is going, even to the point of being willing to risk your life for it. In fact, you need to believe that your very life depends on hitching a ride on that train.

Caution!

Reading this book may be hazardous to your entire belief system. It will cause you to question every belief that you hold, have ever held and will ever hold. Everything that you believe to be true about yourself and about the universe, past, present and future, will be turned inside out and upside down, fed to the shredder and then dumped into the recycling bin.

Also, reading this book will not solve your problems in the world, at least not anytime soon. If you are experiencing serious health, relationship, psychological, financial, personal or any other difficulties, please consider obtaining appropriate professional help. If you are looking for a spirituality that will miraculously make your life good, and fix whatever you perceive to be wrong with the world, move on to the next book on your shelf. This teaching does not aim at fixing the world.

If, on the other hand, you have reached a point in your life where all previous learning has proved unsatisfactory and you are utterly and completely fed up with your struggles in the world and are now sincerely looking for a teaching that is brilliantly logical and will lead you to an experience of clarity of vision, certainty of knowing and unshakable peace, please read on. This path may be for you. However, and this is not said lightly, you must be prepared and, above all, willing to work very, very, very hard. Oh, one more thing, you must be willing to work hard for a very long time! ☺

Okay, such a warning might sound a bit extreme, but it certainly would give the prospective student a fair heads-up! In the end, it is the seeker's sincere desire for an experience of the truth that will provide the motivation to pursue this path. One of my favourite storytellers and long-time *Course in Miracles* teacher, Jon Mundy, tells the story of the Hindu student who one day approached his master where he stood in a river and told him that he wanted to be enlightened. The master reached out, grabbed the student by the neck, plunged his head under water and held it there. The student struggled frantically until, finally, the master released his hold.

When the student finally caught his breath and could again speak, he said, "Why Master, why did you do that?"

The Master asked, "When you were under water, what did you desire more than anything else?"

"More than anything," replied the student, "I wanted to be able to take a breath."

"Then," the Master said, "when you desire to be enlightened as much as you desired a breath of air, you can be enlightened."

Well Known, but Not Necessarily Popular

A Course in Miracles has received much media attention over the last few years, and though it is certainly becoming increasingly well known, it is doubtful that it will join the ranks of the most popular spiritualities, at least not anytime soon. There are a number of reasons for this, including its absolute and uncompromising nature, its dauntingly sophisticated style of writing and its radical message. But, most of all, it is our deeply rooted resistance to hearing its message that will delay its acceptance among the great spiritual traditions of the world, a place that it justly deserves and will no doubt one day hold. The following sections serve to situate the Course with respect to some of the current popular thought systems and to introduce its unique characteristics. Many of these points will be developed in greater detail in subsequent chapters.

First published in 1976, *A Course in Miracles* is a relative newcomer in the world of spirituality, and though many of its basic concepts can be found in the ancient spiritualities and philosophies of the world, in particular Buddhism and Advaita Vedanta, as a modern-day thought system, it is unique in its revolutionary blend of psychology and metaphysics. This considerable work comprises a text nearly 700 pages long, a workbook containing a one-year training program of 365 daily lessons and a 92-page Manual for Teachers. The third edition also includes two pamphlets that were previously published separately: *The Song of Prayer* and *Psychotherapy: Purpose, Process and Practice*. The text contains the necessary theoretical background for working with the lessons and for eventual application; the lessons provide the practice that will facilitate generalization in the student's personal life.

> A theoretical foundation such as the text provides is necessary as a framework to make the exercises in this workbook meaningful. Yet it is doing the exercises that will make the goal of the course possible. An untrained mind can accomplish nothing. It is the purpose of this workbook to train your mind to think along the lines the text sets forth. (W-pI.in.1:1–4)

A Course in Miracles is, as its title indicates, a course, and like all courses, the mastery of its principles will be directly proportional to the time and effort devoted to its study and, above all, since it is a very practical thought system, to its application. Much as you would not be expected to design and build a skyscraper the day after graduating from engineering school, you are not expected to ascend to heaven the day after having completed a first reading of *A Course in Miracles*. Reading the text and doing the workbook lessons is part of the initial preparation work; the journey of the Course student truly begins once application in daily life begins.

Although it can be helpful, it is not necessary to sign up for classes, find a study group, attend workshops or join an online community in order to learn the Course. In fact, sometimes joining with others, especially beginning students, can add to the confusion and delay progress. However, given our natural human propensity for socialization and gathering, many will seek out a group, if only to exchange experiences and ideas. Also, given the radical nature of this thought system, students are likely to find themselves in the awkward situation in which they are pursuing a spirituality that does not find favour among close friends and family members, and so comfort and reinforcement may be obtained by joining a group of like-minded seekers.

A Course in Miracles stands on its own as a complete, self-contained, highly individualized self-study program that can be studied and practised independently of outside support or interaction.

It is also designed in such a way as to lead its students to find their own inner teacher and to develop a learning pace that suits their particular needs. It is a mind-training program that leads to an inner process of release and revelation; it is not a religion or cult. In the end, the Course is for *you*, its student, and can be pursued without any external approval, guidance, support or validation.

How It Came

The contents of the Course came to Dr. Helen Schucman through a process of inner dictation,[1] which she wrote in shorthand, then read back to her colleague, Dr. William Thetford,[2] who typed it up. Both were Professors of Medical Psychology at the Columbia University College of Physicians and Surgeons in New York City. Having struggled for some time with very difficult relationships and constant conflict in the workplace, Bill Thetford one day declared, "There must be a better way and I'm determined to find it." To which Helen replied that he was right and agreed to try the new approach with him. That moment marked an important turning point in their lives—as well as in the lives of many contemporary spiritual seekers—not long after which Helen began to hear the Voice that would dictate what became *A Course in Miracles*.

It is interesting to note that neither Helen nor Bill were engaged in a serious spiritual pursuit at the time of the Course's dictation, which means that it is an appropriate spirituality for any person who seeks peace, with or without prior spiritual training. Also, the Course came to us in one of the world's largest and busiest cities, again, making it a most suitable spiritual path for the active, worldly Westerner. Although *A Course in Miracles* came in response to Helen and Bill's cry for help—since on the deepest level all minds are joined—by extension, it was given in answer to our individual

1. For the definitive and engaging story of Helen Schucman and her scribing of *A Course in Miracles*, see *Absence from Felicity*, by Kenneth Wapnick, PhD

2. For a fascinating and touching account of the life of William Thetford, see *Never Forget to Laugh*, by Carol Howe.

prayers, as well as our collective cry for help. Helen and Bill were the gracious instruments of this most holy gift.

What the Course Shares with Other Spiritualities

Like many spiritual and metaphysical thought systems, *A Course in Miracles* begins with the idea that there is a God, or Source, that is the origin of all creation. It says that we are as God created us, spirit, whole and not lacking for anything; that God is perfect love, perfectly whole, perfectly peaceful and that we are, and always have been, loved by our Father. It leads us on a healing journey, where we are taught to be vigilant for our thoughts, the real source of our difficulties, disquiet, pain, illnesses and loss of peace, similar to the ancient path of Self-enquiry as revived and taught by Sri Ramana Maharshi. Bill Thetford dubbed the Course the "Christian Vedanta" because of its use of Christian language to present the non-dualistic teaching of Advaita Vedanta.[3]

As in the practice of *Samatva*, the Course teaches that there is no hierarchy of illusions, that we are all the same. It teaches that true power resides in the mind's ability to choose, and that we are far more than what we can ever imagine ourselves to be. It tells us that peace is a choice and that love is our natural inheritance. Many students of the Course come to experience greater peace, deeper love and tremendous relief from the anxieties and troubles of the world. Like most spiritualities, it carries a message of hope, love, healing and peace.

How Is the Course Different from Other Spiritualities?

Since we consider ourselves to be sophisticated, educated, intelligent beings with ever-expanding analytical and intellectual capabilities, living in bodies in an increasingly complex world, we need a spirituality that meets us where we believe ourselves to be. To be told that we are one mind in Christ would probably not hold much significance nor stimulate motivation for the spiritual quest for the

---

3. Carol Howe, *Never Forget to Laugh*, page 101.

worldly-minded. In answer to this need, Jesus uses a sophisticated psychological approach in *A Course in Miracles* to lead the student through a process of perceptual and mental re-education or, correction of perception, as it is described in the text. It is designed to gradually awaken us to the truth about our seeming existence in the world. Jesus asks us to take a good honest look at what we believe to be our life in the world in a body. In particular, he wants us to see the absurdity of what we are willing to deem acceptable as God's children. Its ultimate goal is an experience of peace of a lasting kind, an experience that is achieved through the practice of a unique form of forgiveness. The application of its teachings happens in the mind of the student and is not aimed at changing the world. In fact, in Zen-like fashion, it has nothing to do with the world and everything to do with the mind of the student.

> The world you see is the delusional system of those made mad by guilt. Look carefully at this world, and you will realize that this is so. For this world is the symbol of punishment, and all the laws that seem to govern it are the laws of death. Children are born into it through pain and in pain. Their growth is attended by suffering, and they learn of sorrow and separation and death. Their minds seem to be trapped in their brain, and its powers to decline if their bodies are hurt. They seem to love, yet they desert and are deserted. They appear to lose what they love, perhaps the most insane belief of all. And their bodies wither and gasp and are laid in the ground, and are no more. Not one of them but has thought that God is cruel. (T-13. in.2:2–11)

Although *A Course in Miracles* shares many basic concepts with other spiritual thought systems, its message is, in many ways, radically different. One very important feature of this teaching is that it provides refreshingly logical answers to those essential, though usually unanswerable questions such as: Why did God create this world? Why did He give us bodies that break down and die? How could He allow even one child to suffer? How could He play favourites? How could He choose sides in battle? How could He even incite battle? How could God sacrifice His only Son? Why do some people experience scarcity and suffering, while others see nothing but abundance and ease? What is the true origin of this universe?

Most of these questions are addressed in one simple, yet very provocative statement: God did *not* create the world. Which means that, by extension, God did not create us as individual persons in the world. In fact, He does not have anything at all to do with this world, not even the slightest bit of interaction. Basically, God does not know anything about our existence here, including you and me. This means that, if God is real, then this world cannot be real. Though logical, for the beginner student of the Course, this line of thinking is, to say the least, anything but reassuring. For all intents and purposes, our experience tells us all too clearly that we do exist, or is it perhaps that we simply believe that we exist?

While most spiritualities, at least the popular contemporary ones, will focus on trying to change things in the world and make the world a better place, *A Course in Miracles* tells us to not waste time trying to fix the world. To further throw us off our game, it does not say that God wants abundance and joy for us in this world, nor does it say that He wants us to make peace in the world. It does not say that He wants us to discover our truth, our authentic selves or our potential in this world, nor that He needs us to do anything whatsoever for Him in the world. It says that God did not make this world, that this world is not our home and, quite simply, that there is no world.

> This world you seem to live in is not home to you. And some-where in your mind you know that this is true. A memory of home keeps haunting you, as if there were a place that called you to return, although you do not recognize the voice, nor what it is the voice reminds you of. Yet still you feel an alien here, from somewhere all unknown. Nothing so definite that you could say with certainty you are an exile here. Just a per-sistent feeling, sometimes not more than a tiny throb, at other times hardly remembered, actively dismissed, but surely to return to mind again. (W-pI.182.1:1–6)

Any way we look at it, this is the only logical conclusion for all of our questions relating to God's involvement in a world of iniquity and death. A God that expresses Himself through an imperfect world—for truly, this world is anything but perfect—cannot Himself be perfect. An imperfect God cannot therefore be the true God. A perfect God can only create perfection. We, as His creations, must be perfect, yet that is not our experience. This world then must not have been created by God. This world cannot be our true home. What then is this world?

While for eons we have believed in a God that interacts in some way with us and our world, *A Course in Miracles* asks us to consider that perhaps He had nothing at all to do with this world. If this is true, it might actually be a very good thing. This might, in fact, be our only chance for a way out. This would mean that there is hope. This would mean that there is "not this," there is something other than this world of imperfection and, ultimately, death for everything and everyone. This would mean that there can really be peace, wholeness and perfect love; only it is found "not here."

Reawakening the Inquisitive Child

It is interesting to observe how our natural childhood inquisitiveness erodes with age, so that by the time we reach adulthood, we have long stopped asking those silly questions that were once thought to be so cute, until they began to annoy our parents and teachers. Most every child will have wondered where a loved one or favourite pet went after death. Every child has asked *What for?* when told to eat his vegetables or button up his coat before going outside.

Experience eventually showed us that many of the answers we were given made sense. Going outside in the snow without a warm coat led to physical discomfort, so buttoning up before going outside seemed like the smart thing to do. We stopped asking why it gets cold in the winter because that's just the way winter is. The reason for eating broccoli might not have been apparent until later in life when maintaining good health became a more serious concern. We may even have accepted that Bucky the budgie went to heaven to be with Grannie Annie, even though our "What for?" garnered little more than a vague and unsatisfactory "Because that's what happens when someone dies."

As the years passed, we grew up and accepted that sometimes "What for?" didn't really have an answer that made sense, and so we stopped asking. We accepted that God takes good things away from us, all for no apparently logical reason other than that He does what He does because He can. We stopped wondering why God gave us cold winters, what He is doing in heaven with our deceased loved ones and why He made broccoli if no one even likes it. We simply stopped questioning altogether, going along with the answers handed down to us by those who grew up and stopped questioning long before we did. We grew up and became sensible, practical adults.

As students of *A Course in Miracles*, we are asked now to reawaken our sleeping, questioning mind, to look at everything we believe to be true and ask "What for? What is the purpose of this situation or experience?" If we are sad or unhappy or suffering in any way, we are asked to question not only our experiences and our perceptions but also the cause of our experiences. We are invited to look at, and question, every single truth that we hold onto. We are asked to question our very existence. *A Course in Miracles* takes the student on a journey that leaves no stone unturned, not even the tiniest grain of sand.

The Voice of the Course

The name of *Jesus* is the name of one who was a man but saw the face of Christ in all his brothers and remembered God. So he became identified with *Christ*, a man no longer, but at one with God.... It is possible to read his words and benefit from them without accepting him into your life. Yet he would help you yet a little more if you will share your pains and joys with him, and leave them both to find the peace of God. (C-5.2:1–2; 6:6–7)

Jesus is the voice of *A Course in Miracles*. I have heard people express uneasiness with this fact, and many have abandoned its study because of it. Although it is possible to pursue this path without taking advantage of the help offered by Jesus, to push him aside because of the Christian form of his message gives pause for consideration. Such a reaction might indicate a problem with authority, or it might be that the message conveyed by the Course was found to be too threatening to that part of the mind that does not wish to question reality. To say that the Course is not for you because of its association with Jesus could be a convenient escape from the truth.

> Equals should not be in awe of one another because awe implies inequality. It is therefore an inappropriate reaction to me. An elder brother is entitled to respect for his greater experience, and obedience for his greater wisdom. (T-1.II.3:5–7)

On the other side of the coin, to make Jesus into an icon of specialness is just as problematic because it reinforces the belief in separateness, a belief that the Course asks us to look at and reconsider. He presents himself as our older brother and asks only that we give him a chance to help us in our process. He is one who recognized the insignificance of the oasis and found a way out of the desert, one who returned to the Father, one who understood that what we call life is only a dream and that this world is not our true home. He understands the reasons why we think this is our home and why we cannot see our true reality. He stands on the other side, holding out his hand to us and says, "Come with me to where your Father, who has never forgotten you, waits for you." He holds the light so we can find our way out of the darkness. As the Voice of the Course, it only makes sense to defer to his wisdom, to simply follow the teaching he gave us, as it was given. One of my favourite quotes from the Course comes from its early pages:

> There is nothing about me that you cannot attain. I have nothing that does not come from God. The difference between us

now is that I have nothing else. This leaves me in a state that is only potential in you. (T-1.II.3:10–13).

I have reminded myself of these words countless times, their implication being so very far-reaching. This means that in order for us to awaken, as he did, we need simply relinquish that which is not of God. The first order of business then remains for us to identify what is not of God, understand why we so dearly cling to it, acknowledge that it does not give us peace and then, by the grace of the Holy Spirit, release it. It is truly and wonderfully simple, at least in theory. In practice, well, that's why we have hundreds of pages of text and 365 workbook lessons.

Life Is But a Dream

Dreams show you that you have the power to make a world as you would have it be, and that because you want it you see it. And while you see it you do not doubt that it is real. Yet here is a world, clearly within your mind, that seems to be outside. You do not respond to it as though you made it, nor do you realize that the emotions the dream produces must come from you. (T-18.II.5:1–4)

As in many other spiritualities, the Course uses sleep and the dream as a metaphor to help explain why our seeming experience here in this world seems all too real to us. In time, its student comes to the disturbing realization that the idea of the dream is much more than just a metaphor. The truth is that we are indeed very much asleep, and in this state of sleep, we are dreaming. Being in a state of deep sleep, we are unaware of anything outside the dream, and since all of our experiences come from our dreams, we believe this dream world to be true.

Does not a world that seems quite real arise in dreams? Yet think what this world is. It is clearly not the world you saw before you slept. Rather it is a distortion of the world, planned solely around what you would have preferred. (T-18.II.1:1–4)

Throughout the Course, the message that what is true is true and what is not true cannot be true is constantly reinforced. As with every aspect of its teachings, the Course is absolutely consistent, a point that very much simplifies its study and eventual learning. If this world is not our true reality, but our experience leads us to believe that it is real, then we must be dreaming. In dreams, images, figures, situations and dramas seem very real. Dream images and experiences arise from parts of our mind that remain for the most part unconscious. The Course teaches us to look into that part of the mind from which our dream images arise.

> You are at home in God, dreaming of exile but perfectly capable of awakening to reality. Is it your decision to do so? You recognize from your own experience that what you see in dreams you think is real while you are asleep. Yet the instant you waken you realize that everything that seemed to happen in the dream did not happen at all. You do not think this strange, even though all the laws of what you awaken to were violated while you slept. Is it not possible that you merely shifted from one dream to another, without really waking? (T-10.I.2:1–6)

At any moment, the Course teaches, we can awaken from the dream. However, how can we awaken from a dream that we do not even know we are having? The first step in moving from a state of dreaming to a state of waking is to be willing to consider the possibility that we might actually be asleep. This would mean that we are oblivious of our true reality, that we probably do not recall what it is to be awake. The next step is to decide whether we want to remain in the dream, or if we wish to awaken. This is simply a matter of choice.

Finally, if we have decided that we would rather awaken from the dream, then we need something, a beacon, someone who is outside the dream to show us how to awaken. To use means, teachings and guidance that were made up within the dream, such as, for example, the belief systems of the religions of the world, will not likely lead us away from the dream; dream tools were made to keep us in the dream. They may help us dream a happier dream, but they will not awaken us from the dream. Jesus, like the Buddha, is one who awoke from the dream; having done so, he is in a rather good position to help us, in turn, awaken. From his place outside the dream, he calls us, gently, lovingly and patiently to follow him to our true waking state. *A Course in Miracles* is his voice calling to us from outside the dream, it is the hand he extends from the place that is our true home. To take his hand and be led out of the dream is a choice that anyone can make. One only needs to be willing to take his hand and follow the path he has laid out for us in *A Course in Miracles.*

How can you wake children in a more kindly way than by a gentle Voice that will not frighten them, but will merely remind them that the night is over and the light has come? You do not inform them that the nightmares that frightened them so badly are not real, because children believe in magic. You merely reassure them that they are safe now. Then you train them to recognize the difference between sleeping and waking, so they will understand they need not be afraid of dreams. And so when bad dreams come, they will themselves call on the light to dispel them. (T-6.V.2.1–5)

Chapter 3

THE LANGUAGE OF MIRACLES

Oneness is simply the idea God is. And in His Being, He encompasses all things. No mind holds anything but Him. We say "God is," and then we cease to speak, for in that knowledge words are meaningless. There are no lips to speak them, and no part of mind sufficiently distinct to feel that it is now aware of something not itself. It has united with its Source. And like its Source Itself, it merely is. (W-pI.169.5:1–7)

A Language of Its Own

*L*IKE SO MANY STUDENTS of the Course, I found its language daunting. However, though it slowed me down considerably, I refused to allow it to get in the way of my study. Challenging as it was, it was clear that if I were to get anywhere with this spiritual path, I would have to acquire a fairly good grasp of its terminology and concepts. It took nearly four years of diligent study before I began to appreciate that this was, in fact, a simple course, but I first needed to get a handle on how Jesus makes use of otherwise familiar Judeo-Christian language and symbolism to get his unique message across. However, Jesus says that only God is true, and that's it. "Then we cease to speak…" And while he proceeds to tell us that words are meaningless, he spent seven years dictating over half a million words to a scribe in order to get his message across!

This fact alone would make it appear as though the teaching of the Course is complex; yet it claims that quite the opposite is true. Its message is extremely simple, "God is." Everything else is illusion.

Rather, it is because of our extreme resistance to seeing the truth and to accepting its message that we need a training program of more than two words.

> God does not understand words, for they were made by separated minds to keep them in the illusion of separation. Words can be helpful, particularly for the beginner, in helping concentration and facilitating the exclusion, or at least the control, of extraneous thoughts. Let us not forget, however, that words are but symbols of symbols. They are thus twice removed from reality. (M-21.1:7–10)

In heaven, there is no need of words; there is only an experience of perfect oneness. Had I been ready to accept the truth, this book would have ended right here. Obviously, I was not. From my experience, there was an idea of God, but there was an equally valid idea—and experience—of me, in a body, writing a book and doing all sorts of other equally important things in an all-too-real and valid world. That being the case, I would need words, at least for a little while longer. Given my inability to fully comprehend this new message, I would need lots of words! Language is, after all, a means of communicating knowledge and information. In *A Course in Miracles*, Jesus communicates to us a mind-training program, a method for awakening from the dream and returning home. Given that my goal is to awaken from the dream and return home and the Course is designed to achieve this goal, clearly, then, its language I must learn. Though language is necessary for those who experience themselves as separate from God, the goal of the Course is to take us beyond language, to an actual experience of oneness.

A Course in Miracles is written in a sophisticated style of language and form. That is a fact. However, I do not believe that this was done with the intention of excluding those with less sophisticated intellects and education. In its current form, it casts a wider net and is likely to appeal to a broader range of students. It is possible even that those of simpler mind and ready heart may encounter less resistance to its message of non-judgment and shared interests.

They may be more open to setting aside their fear of looking at, and seeing, the truth, willing to trust in the process into which its students are invited, perhaps even finding the journey home far easier and less strewn with resistance and obstacles. Those with more highly polished intellects and greater academic and cultural exposure are likely to find the style and content of the Course challenging and appealing. They will appreciate the flavours of Freud, Plato and Shakespeare, as well as its many references to the traditional religions, philosophies and theologies of the world. Yet, at the same time, the highly intellectual mind may fall into the trap of churning out more elaborate and subtle forms of resistance, delaying, and even preventing, progress along the path.

A few people have expressed displeasure over the pervasive use of the male gender, taking offense with terms such as God the Father, the Son of God and the Sonship. Since *A Course in Miracles* is a purely non-dualistic teaching, it would be counter-productive to inject gender differentiation, a clearly dualistic approach, in its terminology. In heaven, there is only oneness; if there were male and female expressions, then there would be no oneness.

Though I was far from being an academic or cultural genius, I was well aware of the creative power of my mind and its ability to come up with clever and, even at times, ingenious objections and resistance to working with the Course. All the more reason to reinforce my resolve with a thorough understanding of its core teaching. Setting my language concerns aside, I dove in and did my best to understand everything that I needed to make progress with this path. By the same token, I also sensed that it was not necessary to understand every single reference in the book; it is not the form of the teaching that is important, but rather its content. The one essential ingredient for making progress with this spiritual path is willingness. In time, the student eventually learns that no amount of intellectual understanding can replace everyday conscious application of its principles, an exercise that is likely to require great willingness. It is, in the end, a very practical course.

Judeo-Christian Terminology

There is no need of words in heaven, and words are but symbols of symbols. However, I still believe that I am here, in a body, and I need words, at least until experience teaches me otherwise. Talk to me. By the looks of it, I am not alone in this predicament, and in answer to our collective cry for help, Jesus obliged us with this Course. I will not presume to know how decisions were made about how to best help humanity in our time of need, but it would only make sense that if we were to be given a thought system, or a training program for awakening from the dream, then its form and language should be one with which we can relate and, above all, it should be logical and consistent.

> This is a manual for a special curriculum, intended for teachers of a special form of the universal course. There are many thousands of other forms, all with the same outcome. (M-1.4:1–2)

On numerous occasions, I have heard people declare that they were "turned off" by the language of *A Course in Miracles*. For some, it seems far too complicated. Others are resentful because it is too Christian, too religious or too biblical. One man told me that he had been completely turned off because of the overbearing presence of Jesus. Though *A Course in Miracles* was given to all seekers, regardless of spiritual, religious, cultural or philosophical background, it does not claim to be suitable for everyone. It is certainly not the only path and in fact positions itself as one among thousands; the sincere seeker will always be guided to the most suitable path. However, it might be worth considering that objections concerning the form of the Course might very well hide a profound inner resistance to its actual message. That being the case, it would mean that the content of the Course has been perceived as a threat to the false self we so desperately cling to, indicating that a second look might perhaps be worth the extra effort.

A Course in Miracles came to us through Dr. Helen Schucman, a highly intelligent, logical-minded educator and psychologist, and also a great admirer of Shakespeare. Its content came through her in the late sixties and seventies, in English, in New York City. It might have come in any number of forms, from any place in the world, using one or a mixture of the mythologies and symbols of our traditional spiritualities and philosophies. But it came, as it did, in the language of Shakespeare, in a major city of the Western world, to a psychologist of Judeo-Christian background. For the purposes of consistency, it uses the terminology of Christianity and the psychology of the day, resulting in a form with which a great number of people can relate.

At the same time, the Course corrects many of the misunderstandings associated with the original teachings of Jesus and of the Bible and, as necessary, applies entirely new meanings. It also adds depth and perspective to certain basic psychological concepts, providing explanations for motivations and behaviour that we had not yet grasped. To enable communication of its message to its students who have need of words, *A Course in Miracles* was given to us in a logical and consistent form. The Course leads its students to use their personal life as their spiritual classroom. No changes of lifestyle are required, nor are any stringent disciplines imposed. The pace is tailored to the student's lifestyle and, most of all, willingness to progress. If there is one spirituality that is perfectly suited for our frenetic, materialistic, highly individualistic contemporary Western lifestyles, it certainly is *A Course in Miracles*.

A Course in Unlearning

A Course in Miracles is truly a course and, as such, it has a clearly defined curriculum and lesson plan. It is meant to be studied and applied by its students if its goal of learning is to be achieved. It is not a book to be opened at random like some magical oracle consulted to provide momentary inspiration about how to solve a problem in the world. Its principle focus is the training of the mind, something that is achieved through study, practice and application in the everyday situations encountered by its students. Like many programs of study that contain a theoretical component as well as a practical component in the form of lab work, exercises and sometimes even fieldwork, the Course comprises a textbook and a set of daily lessons.

> It is the function of God's teachers to bring true learning to the world. Properly speaking it is unlearning that they bring, for that is "true learning" in the world. (M-4.X.3:6–7)

However, unlike most courses where much of the learning has occurred by the time the curriculum has been completed, the real learning intended by *A Course in Miracles* actually occurs as a process that can take many years after the student has read the book and completed the lessons. Also, unlike other teaching programs, it is not designed to teach anything that we do not already know, or possess. Unlike many other spiritual schools, there is no hierarchy of learning, nor are there degrees of accomplishment or attainment. As such, it should not be approached as knowledge that needs to be acquired.

A Course in Miracles is designed to undo the wrong learning accumulated through a lifetime of experience in a body, in the world. Its goal is to remove that which stands between us and an experience of the truth. The removal of the veil that stands between us and the truth is instantaneous; however, our fear of letting go of our false learning makes it appear difficult to attain. Since the Course uses the student's life as a classroom, learning occurs in a highly individualized manner. With its gentle and slowly evolving learning process, students can, at their own pace, and given their unique life journey, gradually remove the blockages to seeing the truth and eventually find their way home. All of this can be accomplished by studying, learning and applying the teachings contained in the book, and doing so with the help of its teacher, Jesus. No additional outside help or resources are required.

On Teaching and Learning

> Changes are required in the *minds* of God's teachers. This
> may or may not involve changes in the external situation.... By
> far the majority are given a slowly evolving training program,
> in which as many previous mistakes as possible are corrected.
> Relationships in particular must be properly perceived, and all
> dark cornerstones of unforgiveness removed. Otherwise the
> old thought system still has a basis for return. (M-9.1:1–2, 7–9)

When I reached the third part of the book, the Manual for
Teachers, I grew excited at the thought of quitting my business
and becoming a teacher of *A Course in Miracles*. I knew that I still
had a long way to go in my studies before I could ever claim to be
one of its teachers. Nonetheless, this was something I could look
forward to. Then I read more carefully. Jesus was not calling for
teachers of the Course; he was calling for students who were willing to apply its lessons in their lives. It is by applying the teachings
of the Course that we become teachers of its message, referred to
as "teachers of God" in the Manual. In effect, we teach by example.
Becoming a teacher of God has nothing to do with opening up a
school to teach *A Course in Miracles*. In fact, when asked if changes
are required in the life situation of God's teachers, Jesus answers
that, other than in a few rare cases, changes are not likely. I felt
momentarily disappointed, but at the same time relieved of the
tremendous burden of having to really learn the Course. I would
remain a student. That made much more sense, and was simpler.
Furthermore, I would be a silent teacher. No one needed to know
what was going on in my mind. This was actually better. Given my
staunch resistance to undoing my ego identification, it was clear
that I would be in the slowly evolving group.

> The role of teaching and learning is actually reversed in the
> thinking of the world. The reversal is characteristic. It seems as
> if the teacher and the learner are separated, the teacher giving
> something to the learner rather than to himself. Further, the
> act of teaching is regarded as a special activity, in which one

engages only a relatively small proportion of one's time. The course, on the other hand, emphasizes that to teach is to learn, so that teacher and learner are the same. (M-in.1:1–5)

In *A Course in Miracles*, Jesus explains that we have confused teaching and learning, that we are in fact constantly teaching and learning, even while we sleep. This is accomplished on an ongoing basis by the choices we make in our mind. When we choose with the ego, our words and actions will convey a message of separateness, specialness, need, want, fear, scarcity or any number of responses that reflect the thought of separation. When we choose with the thought system of the Holy Spirit, our thoughts and actions will reflect the love and kindness that come from an understanding of shared interests. Jesus asks us to choose with the right mind, in which case, we will teach that there is an alternative to the wrong-minded thought system of separation. Therefore, our teaching and learning functions remain strictly in the mind.

Resign now as your own teacher.... Remember nothing that you taught yourself, for you were badly taught. (T-12.V.8:3; T-28.1.7:1)

Quite early in my work with the Course, I understood that a fair dose of humility would be most helpful in facilitating this learning process. Being the chronic self-taught do-it-yourselfer that I am, to be told that I don't know anything, that my eyes don't see and that my ears don't hear—in fact, that my entire sensory apparatus is little more than a system of deception—was like receiving a bucket of ice water in the face. When I began to reread the Course a second time, it was with the understanding that I really knew nothing. This attitude left me more open to exploring this unusual thought system, making it much easier to resign as my own teacher and to accept Jesus as my new teacher. A huge burden had been lifted from my shoulders. I knew nothing. At least I knew that much. This was good, because what I knew had not brought me the peace of God. There must be a better way of looking at life and the world, and by the looks of it, Jesus knew the way.

On the Confusion of Levels

A major step in the Atonement plan is to undo error at all levels. Sickness or "not-right-mindedness" is the result of level confusion, because it always entails the belief that what is amiss on one level can adversely affect another. We have referred to miracles as the means of correcting level confusion, for all mistakes must be corrected at the level on which they occur. Only the mind is capable of error. (T-2.IV.2:1–4)

When I first started to work with the Course, I instantly felt it was telling me the truth. However, it wasn't long before I saw that my understanding of what was real and what was symbolic was actually completely upside down. I believed the world to be real, and God to be a vague symbol of a pure creative source "out there" somewhere and certainly beyond my reach. But Jesus tells us that only God and His Creations are real; everything else is illusion. This meant that I, this student of the Course—and even the Course itself—belonged to the illusion, since God has nothing to do with this world. Jesus could have said to us simply, God is. Seek only the experience. That would have been the truth. However, it certainly would not have been very helpful, since I perceived myself as being galaxies away from the experience.

"I rest in God." This thought has power to wake the sleeping truth in you, whose vision sees beyond appearances to that same truth in everyone and everything there is. Here is the end of suffering for all the world, and everyone who ever came and yet will come to linger for a while. Here is the thought in which the Son of God is born again, to recognize himself. (W.pI.109.3:3–6)

A Course in Miracles is a spiritual thought system designed to make us see that our existence here—in the world, in bodies—is not our true life. It calls to us from beyond the desert in a language and voice we can hear and understand in the world. It comes from a place where only perfect oneness exists and is given to us who have forgotten that only perfect oneness exists. In fact, we are so embroiled in our seeming experience of separation that we do not even stop to wonder if there exists anything other than separateness. Jesus makes very precise and specific use of our language with the goal of leading us to a point where we can choose differently. To interpret the Course's message in a way that leads us to focus our attention on making changes in the world in order to attain this goal would be a misinterpretation of its message. He wants us to change our *minds*, not to change the world.

The following story illustrates well the approach that Jesus chose to take in order to get his message across to us in a way that would not scare us to death. It is said that after many years of intense searching, while observing a star twinkling in the early morning sky, Sakyamuni Buddha attained enlightenment. In great joy, he cried out, "How wonderful, how wonderful! Everybody is endowed with the wisdom and appearance of Tathagata!" Which is the same as saying, "All beings are primarily Buddhas!" Those who heard him fled the scene in a hurry. "How absurd! We are so sinful, greedy and ill-tempered. How could we be enlightened beings? Don't deceive us." Sakyamuni saw that it might be best to teach according to where people were in their understanding. He began by preaching, "You are sinful creatures and are in defilement. Repent, and purify yourselves. Do good for your future happiness." A little later, he told them, "You all think that there is you, yourselves, and there is the world; there is ignorance and there is enlightenment. However, everything with form changes. Everything in the world is just a result of causes and conditions. The happiness of life is to come to this realization and live with no attachment." In time, the people grew ready to hear what he had to teach, eventually becoming open to hearing the truth.[1]

At first, I was under the impression that Jesus was actually speaking to us in the world, offering to help us, as distinct bodies, to experience peace, joy and healing. He did give us this book, in our language, that throughout addresses us directly, where we think

---

1. Adapted from *A Flower Does Not Talk*, Abbot Zenkei Shibayama.

we are: "you believe... you think... you have... you are... you say... you fear... you feel..." When I understood that he was not even speaking to me, as a person, that he was speaking to the part of my mind that remains hidden from my awareness, I felt a little upset, even angry. But mostly, I felt lost and abandoned. But as I continued to study, I began to appreciate the thought that there exists a Self that is far greater than this illusory self that I believe to be quite real, a Self that is at home with God and enjoys all the favours of God's Love, wholeness and peace. I recognized that this was something that I wanted more than anything else in the world.

If Jesus did not have the appearance of speaking to us here in the world, how could he get through to us? In truth, there is only an experience of oneness, and the only thing that might come close to it from our perspective is the idea of perfect love, which is not even something to be experienced in a body. How can we, who use language to communicate between bodies, possibly understand this concept? When Jesus speaks to us in the world, it is only in order to help us look, so that we may eventually see that this world of separation cannot be our true home. He is trying to draw our attention to a level of mind that we don't even know exists. Respectful of the power of our minds to choose to remain in the desert or to leave it, Jesus speaks to us on our level, with words, as though we were separate bodies. As such, some things are meant to be taken literally and others metaphorically. When Jesus says that nothing happened, that we are at home with God, he means this literally; when he says that God weeps for us and waits for us, he means it metaphorically.

The Miracle

> Miracles occur naturally as expressions of love. The real miracle is the love that inspires them. In this sense everything that comes from love is a miracle. (T-1.I.3:1–3)

The Miracle, as used in *A Course in Miracles*, has nothing at all of the miracle as we commonly know it. We generally look for a miracle when situations are out of control, when we are in the midst of situations that are extreme, dire and utterly hopeless. We pray for a miracle when tragedy strikes our homeland, our town, our family or our body. In praying for a miracle, we are asking for help to relieve us of our pain, our terror, our grief. Throughout history, mankind has had countless, in fact, far too many, reasons to pray for a miracle. Yet, in our prayers, for what exactly have we prayed? Relief from pain and terror? Peace? Yet, have we ever really considered *the cause* of our pain? Our lack of peace? Our terror? We have only been aware of something happening to us.

Following the tragic events of September 11, 2001, I was inspired to write an article for my blog. This was written at a time in my life when, having lost faith in all things religious and spiritual, I had effectively blocked God out of my life. Yet, during this time of tragedy, like so many millions of people around the world, I looked for a miracle. Little did I know that one day, I would come to know true miracles.

In Search of a Miracle

As I tried to reconcile the events of this past week, I found that I was unable to find solace in my faith. For, you see, over the past several years, my faith had dwindled to a faint belief in a Universal force, that may or may not be compassionate, that may or may not even care what we did or did not do.

As of late, my faith in humanity had also begun to fade. I thought of the senseless wars that tarnish our past and our present, of our persistent disregard for life and for nature, of how we have used our creativity and inventiveness to develop weapons of mass destruction, of our lack of consideration for one another, and then I wondered how God could possibly love such as us.

I realized this week that I had grown to resent the God of my childhood learning. How could I believe in a God that consistently refrained from interceding in man's affairs, no matter how great a horror we brought to bear upon our brothers and sisters? As I watched the service at the Cathedral in Washington this morning and then in other cities around the world, I thought that this would be a good time for a miracle. Mary, who hears the prayers of God's children, where are you now? Why not appear in this church, in front of all these people who are praying for help and guidance? Why is it that we never see miracles in convincing ways?

And so I searched deep within for that spark of faith that would help me come to terms with the fact that neither God nor Saint seemed inclined to help mankind in our hour of need. And it dawned on me that the miracle was not to be sought above, but below. The miracle lies in the fact of our very existence, in our survival through centuries of struggle against natural and man-made adversity. In our continued faith in ourselves, and yes, in our faith in God.

And I thought of the miracle of this body, which is the temple of my soul and which has borne two wonderful beings. I thought of the miracle of the fire from the candles that burned nearby, taking the chill out of the air around me. I thought of the miracle of man's creativity, such as expressed in Mozart's *Requiem* that filled the room as I wrote these words. I thought of the courage of the individuals who had worked day and night this week in the hope of saving a life amidst ruin and devastation. I thought of the outpouring of love and support from around the world, and of the multi-faith services held in cities around the world today.

In my separateness from God, I had forgotten that we are a part of God's creation, and no matter how infinitely small a part we be, we remain one with God, and as such, God loves each of us just as we love each of our children. In thinking of all that humanity had accomplished despite lack of direct intervention from God, and in spite of our own errant ways, I came to realize that we are the miracle.

In giving us *A Course in Miracles*, Jesus answered our prayers. He gave us what we needed; he gave us what we asked for. He gave us a miracle; the miracle of truth. He gave us a thought system that would once and for all deliver us from all of our pain, suffering, loss and grief. He gave us a thought system that pointed to the cause of our pain, suffering, loss and grief. The miracle Jesus offers us gives us an experience of unshakable, everlasting peace, wholeness, healing and complete abundance. The miracle shows us the way to our true home. The miracle uncovers our innocence. The miracle opens us up to receiving the Love of God.

The miracle of the Course goes well beyond any miracle we could ever imagine, including miracles of healing and raising the dead. The miracle Jesus offers leads to our leaving the desert, to waking from the dream and returning to our true home in heaven with God. The miracle undoes the mistake, the original error, the silly thought that says that it is possible to be separate from perfect oneness. The miracle has many possible forms of expression, because the circumstances of our lives appear to be varied, complex and numerous. But once understood, the miracle is simple, natural and well within our reach. In fact, the miracle is our true nature.

> There is no order of difficulty in miracles. One is not "harder" or "bigger" than another. They are all the same. All expressions of love are maximal.... Miracles are natural. When they do not occur something has gone wrong. (T-1.I.1:1–4; 6:1–2)

The Miracle Occurs When...

The Miracle occurs when I choose to see another's
interests as being not separate from my own.

The Miracle occurs when I look at a situation and
forgive my brother for what he has not done.

The Miracle occurs when I choose to accept responsibility for how
I see things, for how I interpret circumstances, and for how I feel.

The Miracle occurs when I understand that what is
outside is simply a picture of what is inside myself.

The Miracle occurs when I forgive myself
for my misinterpretations.

The Miracle occurs when I look with the Holy Spirit.

The Miracle occurs when I look without judgment.

The Miracle occurs when I can take something
from the teachings of *A Course in Miracles* and
apply it in my life so that healing can occur.

Pauline Edward
May 2010

Chapter 4

MAN, MYTH AND MIRACLES

There is another way of looking at the world.

Since the purpose of the world is not the one I ascribed to it, there must be another way of looking at it. I see everything upside down, and my thoughts are the opposite of truth. I see the world as a prison for God's Son. It must be, then, that the world is really a place where he can be set free. I would look upon the world as it is, and see it as a place where the Son of God finds his freedom. (W-pI.57.3:1–6)

A Steep Learning Curve

*B*EFORE BEING INTRODUCED TO *A Course in Miracles*, I had spent years scouring the spiritual buffet line in search of the truth about the nature of existence, in search of answers that made sense, in search of a teaching that would make me feel good about myself, something that would make life worth living. I searched for a thought system I could work with, one I could actively apply in my life. In all my searching, never did I imagine that the one thought system that would make the most sense would end up saying the exact opposite of everything I had been taught, everything I had ever believed to be true. In fact, after a couple of years of intensive study, *A Course in Miracles* left me feeling anything but good about myself, and probably even worse about the world. Were it not for its absolutely brilliant logic, I don't think I would have continued down this path. Despite the fact that it had turned my lifelong beliefs completely upside down, or perhaps because it had, there was no doubt in my mind that the Course was painting for me a picture of the truth. Nothing else had ever made this much sense, and though it was unlike anything else I had encountered, I sensed that it was my only hope. But I would need a miracle to learn to work with this bold new teaching.

> This is a very simple course. Perhaps you do not feel you need a course which, in the end, teaches that only reality is true. But do you believe it? When you perceive the real world, you will recognize that you did not believe it. (T-11.VIII.1:1–4)

When I first began to read the Course, I was lucky if I could get the gist of its message, and what little I did manage to capture was so abstract and outrageously different from everything I had been taught that it was impossible to apply in my daily life. The knowledge that this world—that my life—was nothing but an idle dream was too esoteric. How could the idea of this world as a dream help me deal with those situations that appeared all too real to me? I would need a stronger grasp of this radical new message if it was going to be of any use. Being more of a mechanic than an academic, I would have preferred to skip over the study part of the process and get right down to the business of its practical application, but, much as I tried, there was no way I could ever successfully practise a thought system of which I grasped only its gist. There was no way around it: if I were to make progress with the Course, I would have to brave its steep learning curve and acquire a solid understanding of its metaphysical and psychological foundations. The practical application would come afterwards.

> There is no world! This is the central thought the course attempts to teach. Not everyone is ready to accept it, and each one must go as far as he can let himself be led along the road to truth.... There is no point in lamenting the world. There is no point in trying to change the world. It is incapable of change because it is merely an effect. But there is indeed a point in changing your thoughts about the world. Here you

are changing the cause. The effect will change automatically. (W-pI.132.6:2-4; W-pI.23.2:2–7)

The metaphysics of *A Course in Miracles* was no doubt the biggest pill to swallow. The first hurdle would be to accept the Course's radical basic premise that says that God did not create the world, that He doesn't know about this world and that the world is not even real. Furthermore, my seeming experience here in the world, in a body, is little more than a dream. However, from where I stood, I existed, I was here in the world—monthly bills piled up on my desk to prove it—in an aging body, with aches and pains as ever-present daily reminders. It would take a whole lot of convincing to make me see otherwise.

Starting at the Beginning

Back in high school, my favourite subject was mathematics. While all the other subjects seemed complicated and convoluted, mathematics was orderly, logical and very straightforward. It seemed that it was the only subject I could excel at, given my linear-thinking mind. In my final year of high school, in addition to the usual school board curriculum, our advanced math class was assigned an experimental textbook, which I recall as Kelly math, probably named after its author. While I never understood what was special about Kelly math, from the very start, I eagerly took on the challenge of completing every assigned problem. My biggest thrill was to successfully complete the advanced-level problems. It didn't matter that these were optional; I simply enjoyed the challenge, and, in particular, the satisfaction of finding the solutions.

I happily spent countless late nights consuming gallons of Earl Grey tea while working out complex algebraic equations. When I reached an impasse and felt that I could go no further in resolving an equation, I called on my dad's expertise, but only as a last resort. My dad was an engineer and, though I knew he really enjoyed helping me with my math, by the time I had decided to go to him for help, I had usually run out of steam and, of course, patience. It was always with a sense of abject resignation that I would walk into his room, knowing that my patience would be tested beyond its limits. You see, my dad had this incredibly annoying way of teaching. Coming from a much higher level of mathematics, he would drill the problem down to its essential components. For every single equation that needed solving, we started at the very beginning. Back we went to Algebra 101! By the time I brought a problem to him, usually believing myself to be just one line away from the solution, I was very eager for that tiny little input that would give me the answer. But no! Back to the beginning we went, each and every time.

Of course, knowing that my dad would come through and I would be rewarded with my answer, I checked my impatience and saw the process through to the solution. Despite that this pedagogical approach irritated me to no end, it did teach me to solve complex algebraic equations on my own. Needless to say, I did exceptionally well in my math finals, and, at a time of my life when I found it difficult to find my place in what seemed like a world of chaos, my success with mathematics was a tremendous boost to my fledgling self-esteem.

One Problem, One Solution

> A problem cannot be solved if you do not know what it is. Even if it is really solved already you will still have the problem, because you will not recognize that it has been solved. This is the situation of the world. The problem of separation, which is really the only problem, has already been solved. Yet the solution is not recognized because the problem is not recognized. (W-pI.79.1:1–5)

When it came time to apply the decidedly complex teachings of *A Course in Miracles* in my life, I found it very helpful to use the same pedagogical approach my dad had used so many years earlier. Only, in theory, *A Course in Miracles* is much simpler than Kelly math in that it states that, in truth, there is only one problem and one solution. There are no complex equations to be analyzed and resolved; only one problem, one solution. *A Course in Miracles* teaches that the problem is that we have chosen to believe in the impossible, the solution being that we can, at any time, choose to see the truth. Contrary to our experience, there are not thousands upon thousands of issues and situations to be resolved in the world. Furthermore, it states that the truth has never left us; it has simply been deeply buried and forgotten. It has been there all along. We do not even need to learn anything; we only need to unlearn what is not true. One problem, one solution. What could be simpler? Well, that's about where the simple part of the Course stopped, at least in my understanding. I still hadn't the foggiest idea of what to do with that knowledge, so I would have to start at the beginning.

Non-dualism

What is the starting point of *A Course in Miracles*? Despite my misgivings about the complexity and abstract nature of the subject, I thought it might be best to start with the Course's metaphysics in order to establish the parameters and the foundation of this strange and unusual spirituality. Metaphysics is defined as "the branch of philosophy that deals with the first principles of things, including such concepts as being, knowing, substance, essence, cause, identity, time, and space."[1] This sounded like a good place to start.

A Course in Miracles is unique in that it proposes a thought system that is absolutely *non-dualistic*. It states that what is true is that God is. Period. It states that God is perfect oneness; what God creates is one with God. Being a non-dualistic system, this means that nothing else can be real; nothing outside of perfect oneness can exist. Essentially, the Course teaches that God is perfect oneness, eternal, whole and undivided. If only perfect oneness exists, nothing can be distinct and separate from God, so anything that is not of God cannot be real. Contrary to the non-dualism of Advaita Vedanta, in which it is believed that everything is a form assumed by Spirit, in *A Course in Miracles*, God does not interact with the

---

1. *Canadian Oxford Dictionary.*

world in any way. In fact, it states clearly that there *is* no world; there cannot be anything that is real *and* outside of perfect oneness. The truth is that only God is true and everything else is not true. End of story.

This radical new knowledge was a whole lot of unusual, abstract theory for a non-holy, non-academic, former God-fearing Catholic such as myself to absorb, and it left a huge gap between what the Course says is the truth—what I sensed *must* be true—and my experience in the world in a body. Though undeniably logical, this line of thought was at once intriguing and frightening. It would require closer examination. If we are as God created us, if we are whole and loved, then why is this not our experience? Why do we experience ourselves in bodies—*as bodies*—each distinct one from the other? This world is anything but an expression of oneness and wholeness; this is a world of multiplicity. In fact, we live in a culture that promotes and even idolizes uniqueness. If only oneness is true, then what is this complex world with which we are so fascinated and even completely captivated? If this is not our home, what is our true home? Where is our true home? What incredible thing happened to make us accept a world that is *not* our true home?

> Into eternity, where all is one, there crept a tiny, mad idea, at which the Son of God remembered not to laugh. In his forgetting did the thought become a serious idea, and possible of both accomplishment and real effects. (T-27.VIII.6:2–3)

The Course explains that from that place in eternity where all is one for—in truth, there is only oneness—there occurred a kind of what-if idea, nothing more than a passing notion, an idle thought that disappeared as soon as it seemed to appear. It was as though a part of the one Mind could momentarily entertain the notion "What if I separated myself from my source?" or "What if I could be separate from total abundance? What if I could be something other than perfect oneness? What if I could be something other than all-encompassing love?" It was nothing more than a fleeting thought, gone as quickly as it appeared, a reflection on something that could never occur anyways, since how could anyone or anything actually be separate from perfect oneness? How could anyone or anything *be* what it is not?

> If this were the real world, God *would* be cruel. For no Father could subject His children to this as the price of salvation and *be* loving. (T-13.in.3:1–2)

In considering the possibility that God did not create this world, the question naturally arises, "Then what, or who, did?" If God did not put us here, if God did not even make this world, then what did happen? How could the seemingly impossible have happened? However, to answer this question as it has been posed implies the acceptance as fact that this world was actually created and is therefore real. If we ask, "Who created the world?" or "How was the world created?," we are starting with the assumption that there is actually a world that was created, and therefore this kind of question imposes limits on the answer. Our answer must follow from the basic premise that there is actually a world, which is what our philosophers, scientists and thinkers have done since the dawn of time.

> All questions asked within this world are but a way of looking, not a question asked.... A pseudo-question has no answer. It dictates the answer even as it asks. Thus is all questioning within the world a form of propaganda for itself.... An honest question is a learning tool that asks for something that you do not know. It does not set conditions for response, but merely asks what the response should be. (T-27.IV.4:1; 5:1–3, 6–7)

On the matter of *who* or *what* created the world, *A Course in Miracles* is unique among spiritualities, philosophies and metaphysical thought systems in that it says flatly that *there is no world*, and so we must ask our question from a point that is beyond or outside of the presumed existence of the world. A better question might be, "What then *is* this world?" or "What is this seeming experience in a world that appears to be all too real?" Why do we seem to be experiencing ourselves as bodies, in a world of form? If only what is real exists, then why do we have no memory of what is real?

Rather than waste hundreds of pages pondering the impossible, the simple truth of the matter, the Course tells us, is that nothing happened. Nothing. No more, no less. There is one quality about the Course that stands out above all others and that is that it is truly absolute. It does not waffle in its statements, offering half-truths for one person or occasion, other half-truths elsewhere. It is clear, concise, unconditional and refreshingly absolute and unequivocal in its message. It is probably this very quality, no doubt combined with dogged persistence, that would enable me to navigate through the very clever entangling and confusing objections that my ego would place on my path as I struggled to remove the barriers to my understanding of the truth.

A Myth for Our Times

In my early work with the Course, my reaction was, as told in *Making Peace with God*, that I had about as much use for the Course's myth of creation as I'd had fifty years earlier with the biblical story of Adam and Eve. However, on closer examination, it became clear that the myth of creation of my childhood actually reflected some of my deepest beliefs about myself and my existence. In fact, the belief in sin, as depicted in Adam and Eve's disobedience of God's direct order, and the subsequent feelings of guilt over having been caught in the act, were completely overshadowed by the generalized fear that was my guiding force throughout childhood and a fair portion of my adult life. It isn't that I had no use for the myth of Adam and Eve, but rather that the picture it painted of my inner beliefs was such an accurate depiction of my deepest, hidden motives, that I had no choice but to bury it. *A Course in Miracles* presents its metaphysics by painting a similar mythical picture, but its purpose is entirely opposite to that of the Bible. In fact, the myth of the Course proposes the only hopeful alternative to the otherwise never-ending cycle of birth-sin-guilt-fear-struggle-punishment-death built into the Adam and Eve story, as is also found in the Hindu concept of Samsāra.

Some twenty-five years ago, a channeller told me that I would one day write a book on spirituality and mythology. At the time, I found the idea to be totally unlikely, even preposterous, since anything that was not "reality-based" seemed completely beyond the grasp of my practical brain. Not a great fan of extreme science fiction or fantasy, I had always preferred "real life" stories, so I did not see myself writing on mythology or even spirituality, for that matter. My understanding of what is real and what is fiction was severely put into question when I began to give serious thought to some of the ideas the Course was proposing. From this bold new perspective, everything that is not of God is made up, therefore, not real. I was being taught that this "I", with which I totally identified, did not even exist. However, to be told that I am at home with God and that I am spirit was not very practical information. I was clearly worlds away from understanding how I could go from this world, which I believed and experienced to be all too real, to an "other" real world referred to in the Course, which was supposed to be my *real* real world. So then, what is this world?

In most, if not all, of his workshops and books, Ken Wapnick relates a wonderful mythological representation of the metaphysics of *A Course in Miracles*. Since it did not look like I was going to be able to apply the Course's teachings in my everyday life without a thorough understanding of its metaphysics, I decided to take a closer look with the help of its mythology. A myth is defined as "a widely held but false notion; a fictitious person, thing, or idea,"[2] which, according to Jesus, includes pretty much everything that is of this world, including what I believe to be this self. So much for my perception of myself as a grounded, practical, individual. Myths can be very helpful in explaining events or processes that would otherwise be difficult to express in practical terms, and they are found in all the ancient religions of the world. They tell a story,

2. *Canadian Oxford Dictionary.*

The Tiny Mad Idea

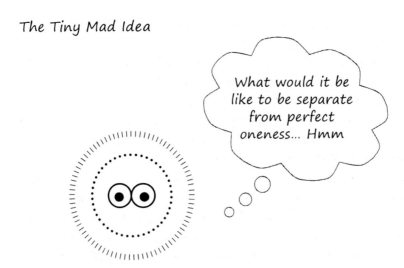

using images that convey feelings, impressions and messages with which we can relate. Given that I believe myself to be in a body, in a world that is all too real to be ignored, this had better be a good story. Actually, make that *the* greatest story ever told!

As much a fan of "reality" as I was, I quickly grew to appreciate the myth of the Course, finding it to be most helpful in getting around some of its more radical metaphysical concepts. In answer to the age-old question, "What is the origin of life?," *A Course in Miracles* proposes an alternative to the Judeo-Christian Adam and Eve myth of creation. By using a what-if scenario, it says that, filled with creative potential and, at the same time, without ever really leaving his Source, the Son of God momentarily entertains the possibility that there might actually be life outside of the Mind of God, a life outside of wholeness, complete abundance and perfect love. The Son seems to have a thought that is outside the Mind of God. If this were actually possible, then perfect oneness would no longer be perfect, so in truth, nothing really happens and the Son of God remains at home in God. In other words, this remains nothing more than a tiny mad idea that disappeared as quickly as it arose.

Since Heaven, or Reality, is a condition of perfect oneness, separation cannot actually occur; whatever does not reflect perfect

Decisions, Decisions...

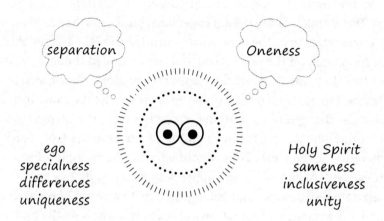

separation   Oneness

ego   Holy Spirit
specialness   sameness
differences   inclusiveness
uniqueness   unity

oneness can only reflect a world of unreality, or a dream state. The Son of God chooses to explore the idea of being an individual. The thought of being distinct, unique and separate from God seems appealing, at least on the surface. There seems to be a self and there is God. But the Son could never actually *be* separate from God, since God is perfect oneness and he is one with God. This remains little more than a passing idea, nothing more than a daydream—besides, how can an idea ever leave its source—the mind? As long as there is God and perfect oneness, there cannot be separateness; since perfect oneness is eternal, it can never stop being what it is. The ability to make a choice between perfect oneness and separateness reflects a dualistic principle, and given that only perfect oneness is true, it too can only be illusory. The Son of God must be dreaming.

Enchanted with the idea of being distinct from God, the Son chooses separation, and since power resides in the mind, this decision necessarily has consequences. Being in a state of choosing, thinking there is actually a choice to be made—perfect oneness or "not perfect oneness"—the mind of the Son becomes split. Where there is choice, there is more than one thing from which to choose and hence duality emerges. Where there is duality, oneness no longer exists. Duality and oneness cannot coexist. Having chosen separation, the memory of oneness fades from awareness; though not destroyed, it is forgotten, buried deep in the mind of the Son.

This thought of separation engenders, on the one hand, what the Course refers to as the ego's wrong-minded thought system of separation, and, on the other hand, the right-minded thought system of the Holy Spirit in which resides the memory of oneness, also referred to as the principle of the Atonement. At the same instant that the thought of separation seemed to occur, the correction for that thought was placed in the mind of the Son, the Holy Spirit's memory of the truth. Now identified with the thought of separation, the Son can no longer appreciate oneness; he has become a separate self, distinct and belonging now to a world of separation and differentiation. Separation has become his new reality and, no longer remembering having chosen separation, oneness is lost from his awareness.

But the ego knows that at any time the Son can look inside and recall that he has the power to make a different choice—with the right mind—and should he remember his true self and accept the Atonement, he would simply return to his true condition of perfect oneness. The choice for oneness would spell the end of separation, hence the end of the ego. Concerned solely with its own survival, the ego must make certain that the Son never makes that choice, so it makes up a very convincing story. It tells the Son that, yes, he has indeed accomplished the impossible, he has separated from his Source. However, since there cannot be anything outside of perfect oneness, in order to have a separate life, the Son had to steal it from God. Given that the nature of perfect oneness is essentially non-dualistic, it's him, or it's God, but it cannot be both. By all appearances, in order to exist as a separate being, the Son had to kill off God!

> You need not fear the Higher Court will condemn you. It will merely dismiss the case against you. There can be no case against a child of God, and every witness to guilt in God's creations is bearing false witness to God Himself. Appeal everything you believe gladly to God's Own Higher Court, because

it speaks for Him and therefore speaks truly. It will dismiss the case against you, however carefully you have built it up. The case may be fool-proof, but it is not God-proof. (T-5.VI.10:1–6)

The ego's story makes sense to the separated Son. Believing he is guilty of a terrible crime, what the Course calls sin, the Son now has a really big problem. God won't be happy; in fact, He is no doubt going to come after him to exact the punishment that is his due. Having lost touch with the memory of his true home with God, the Son, believing himself to be a horrible sinner, capable of an unspeakable crime, comes down with a serious case of guilt. Even worse, as he certainly deserves to be punished, he now fears for his life.

Having forgotten that he has a mind with the ability to make a different choice and no longer able to hear the voice of the Holy Spirit, the Son is completely oblivious to the truth of his innocence. Desperate for help, he turns to the ego, who is only too eager to oblige. Quite pleased to be able to keep the Son in the dark, away from his mind, the ego grabs the Son's attention with an incredible fool-proof plan, a plan that remains just as unreal as the ongoing dream. "I'll make up a world," the ego says, "a special place in which you can hide from God." In need of a solution to his problem, the Son thinks this over. That part of his mind that can make the choice between the Real World and a world of illusion having now been buried deep in the unconscious, he is unaware that his problem is really non-existent and that he has another choice. All he wants now is to be rid of the dreadful sin, guilt and fear that hang over him like a death sentence and the ego's solution seems to make sense. Besides which, he believes that he has no other options.

As promised, the ego makes up a world in which the Son can hide. At the same time, a veil of forgetfulness falls over him so that he can never go back to that place in his mind where he can choose differently. This ensures that the Son will remain mindless, an essential component to the ego's scheme. To really make certain that the Son never takes a serious look inside, the ego, again looking after its own best interests, gives the Son a very fascinating device—a human body with a brain and sensory apparatus. The Son becomes a perceiver. This body, with all its special needs—air, water, food, emotional comfort, material comfort—will keep the Son so busy that he will never stop to wonder if there is anything else. Having totally forgotten that his true home is in heaven, with God, the Son believes himself to be in a body—in fact, he now believes that he *is* a body and his home is the world.

And it all seems to work. This body and this world, at times threatening, at times pleasing, keep the Son so preoccupied that he, in fact, doesn't even have the time to ponder his real origins. It's a full-time job just staying alive! For one, he has to breathe, then he has to eat, then he has to find shelter. This bodily experience is a never-ending proposition. Then there are all the emotional and psychological needs: companionship, love, acceptance, belonging, approval… the list is endless. Believing himself to be a separate individual, the Son constantly struggles with feelings of emptiness, a symbol of the original thought of separation from the wholeness of heaven. He must now work hard to fill this lack by seeking love, affection, food, friendship and possessions in the world outside himself.

Always ready to be of service, in order to help the Son deal with the feelings of loss and also to address the deeply buried thoughts of sin, guilt and fear that will sooner or later resurface, the ego generously provides him with millions upon millions of people and things, ideal for projecting his nasty feelings. "That way," the ego plots, "you'll be innocent, and God won't come after you. He'll go after all those other guilty people, and you'll be safe." The Son, now thinking with the ego and having no memory of the Holy Spirit's right-minded thought system, nor of his true home in heaven, likes very much being a separate individual. So what if there is hunger, pain or suffering, as long as he gets to be distinct and special! Besides, when he suffers, it's not really his fault, it's the body that is hungry or his enemy inflicting pain. He didn't ask to be born; his parents brought him into the world. It's never his fault. This proves that he didn't really do anything wrong. What a trip!

In order to keep the whole separation system spinning, the Son needs to maintain all these other bodies distinct from himself. The ultimate experience of separateness is expressed in special relationships, which include parents, siblings, children, spouses, bosses, friends and enemies. In fact, special relationships provide a great two-for-one bonus. By cleverly manipulating the special people in his life, the now seemingly separated Son gets to have some of his many needs met. At the same time, he has handy targets onto which he can project his anger, frustration, resentment—all manifestations of the deeply repressed original thoughts of sin, guilt and fear that must inevitably rise to the surface, but of which he remains oblivious. Of course, the special people in his life will never entirely meet his needs since his true need is to awaken from the dream and return home, the memory of which remains hidden from his awareness. As a final stroke of genius, having caught onto the ego's way of thinking, the Son invents thought systems and religions that make God the cause of this world. Now it's really not his fault. By the same token, if the whole mess is out of his hands, now there really is no hope of returning home. The Son is doomed to a seeming existence in a make-believe world created by a vengeful, wrathful god.

Making Sense of Myths

If, as *A Course in Miracles* so plainly states, this world—in fact, this entire universe—is not real, then, whatever theory, supposition, premise, hypothesis or story we use to explain how it works, what it is and how it came about, whether theological, philosophical, psychological or scientific, ancient or modern, is myth. This means that this version of the myth of creation, inspired by the thought system given to us by Jesus in *A Course in Miracles*, though different from any other myth in that it does not attribute the creation of the world and the universe to a supreme being or power, is as valid as any, and equally worth serious consideration.

Despite what most of us in the West have been taught, I have heard many people express how difficult it is to reconcile the contradictory representations of God as found in our traditional religions. He is supposed to be a loving Father, but He favours certain people over others. He is wrathful and vengeful and incites killing and war. Also, if He is perfect, how could He have created an imperfect world? Some people see the hand of God in the beautiful things of this world. This raises the question, "If He can take the time to create a beautiful sunset, why would He not take the time to feed the hungry and heal the sick? If there is such a God who has a hand in the making of this world, why will 25,000 children die by the end of this day and every day thereafter?"

To make sense of a story that is clearly insane, it is helpful to look at the traditional Biblical story of creation as a mythical representation of our hidden belief in sin, guilt and fear and a device for keeping us from tapping into the hidden part of our minds rather than as an account of something that actually happened. A loving God could not have created this world and all things in it. If there is a loving, perfect God, He is clearly neither *in* nor *of* this world. This use of myth to explain the origins of our world helped me to disentangle my mind from what was a very unsatisfactory story to begin with. But it was just the beginning of understanding; the application was yet to come.

> There is nothing outside you. That is what you must ultimately learn, for it is the realization that the Kingdom of Heaven is restored to you. For God created only this, and He did not depart from it nor leave it separate from Himself. The Kingdom of Heaven is the dwelling place of the Son of God, who left not his Father and dwells not apart from Him. Heaven is not a place nor a condition. It is merely an awareness of perfect Oneness, and the knowledge that there is nothing else; nothing outside this Oneness, and nothing else within. (T-18. VI.1:1–6)

Chapter 5

THE MEANING OF LIFE IN THE DESERT

> You are the dreamer of the world of dreams. No other cause
> it has, nor ever will. Nothing more fearful than an idle dream
> has terrified God's Son, and made him think that he has lost
> his innocence, denied his Father, and made war upon himself.
> (T-27.VII.13:1–3)

Resistance on the Journey

*P*SYCHOLOGY IS THE STUDY of human motivation and
behaviour, and since we believe ourselves to be distinct, separate individuals living in a world that, as we are now being told, is all made up, we would be remiss in our efforts if we were to pursue a course of study designed to lead us out of the world of dreams without first looking at the cause and, more importantly, the purpose of our dreaming. Jesus states that our seeming existence in the world is simply the result of a mistaken choice and that, at any time, we can awaken from the dream. In order to uncover the cause of our making this choice in the first place, a good place to begin is with an examination of our deepest beliefs about ourselves as psychological beings. In a review of *A Primer of Psychology According to A Course in Miracles* by Joe Jesseph, which I wrote for *Miracles Magazine*, I stated that:

> My own knowledge of psychology is limited to the pop psychology of daytime television and a college level Introduction to Psychology Course that might have been more appropriate

for veterinary students, given that, in my tortured recollection, it seemed to say more about Skinner's rats and Pavlov's dogs than about the human mind. Since this is a primer of psychology, I presume that this book is addressed to students of *A Course in Miracles*, such as myself, with little or no formal training in psychology. Although *A Course in Miracles* does not require that its students acquire a PhD in psychology (even though it may appear so, at least in the early stages of its study), an understanding of certain basic psychological mechanisms belonging to the human psyche is essential for the serious student wishing to make progress on this spiritual path.

But when I set out to further explore and put into words my learning and understanding of the core psychological principles of *A Course in Miracles*, I felt resistance. A part of me did not want to study this subject any more than necessary. In fact, right from the beginning of my work with the Course, a part of me wanted to altogether overlook its bleak psychological teachings, especially the unholy trinity of sin, guilt and fear, hoping that I could just skip ahead to the good parts. However, I soon learned that *A Course in Miracles* engages its students in a very complete process, and to apply it partially would only lead to partial results. Going halfway home was not an option. If I was going to undertake this journey, it would be all the way home, rough patches and smooth parts equally accepted.

Teach only love, for that is what you are.... Light and joy and peace abide in me.... I am as God created me.... I am one Self, united with my Creator.... The name of God is my inheritance. (T-6.III.2:4; W-pI.93, 94, 95, 184)

Throughout *A Course in Miracles*, there are many wonderfully inspiring statements attesting to our true nature as members of God's Creation and it is tempting for the Course student to focus on these while overlooking those that are less flattering. No one really wants to read about the darkness that lurks beneath the surface. However, in order to reach the unchanging light of truth that lies buried deep within, it is necessary to first walk through the seeming darkness that covers it up.

> You see yourself as a ridiculous parody of God's creation; weak, vicious, ugly and sinful, miserable and beset with pain. Such is your version of yourself; a self divided into many warring parts, separate from God, and tenuously held together by its erratic and capricious maker, to which you pray. It does not hear your prayers, for it is deaf. It does not see the oneness in you, for it is blind. It does not understand you are the Son of God, for it is senseless and understands nothing. (W-pI.95.2:1–5)

However, since the purpose of the Course is not to flatter us with pretty phrases about a holiness we clearly do not believe we possess but rather to awaken us to our true nature, Jesus must contrast the truth with our false beliefs. Because we harbour deeply hidden and powerfully crippling beliefs about ourselves, he gives us a program of study that takes us on a gradual process of true Self discovery. It is only by acknowledging and then looking at the darkness that we can awaken from the dream and return to our true home. To ignore the darkness of the desert will only strengthen its hold on us.

Whether or not we are aware of it, because we believe we are vulnerable, that we can be attacked, that what we call our lives can be threatened, delving into a spirituality that is designed to undo our deepest beliefs about ourselves will inevitably stir up great fear and is likely to cause resistance. When it came time for me to work on this chapter, I encountered tremendous resistance. It took days before I actually settled down at the computer, finding numerous more important chores to do over and above my usual consultations and daily activities, such as, moving the bird feeder in my backyard away from the flower bed where the squirrels were happily digging for fallen seeds dangerously close to the lilies—my favourite flowers, their favourite food. Then there was laundry, washing the car, cleaning out the garden shed, shopping, watering the grass, more shopping, performing a security update and backup of my website—all of which were necessary, to a certain extent—interestingly, all of which I did without the least bit of resistance.

It took nearly a week before I managed to sit down in the garden with my laptop, cup of tea and reference notes and materials. It was a beautiful, warm and sunny late April day, and I had been very much looking forward to writing in the garden. I turned on the computer, opened the files and then, within no more than two minutes, fell asleep in the chair. When I awoke, feeling refreshed and recharged, I returned to my laptop only to become obsessed with the fonts in my document. It didn't matter that I had been working with these same fonts for two years: on that day, when I was ready to explore the psychology of *A Course in Miracles*, I decided that I needed to install the proper fonts. The substitute fonts were no longer acceptable.

Once the fonts were installed, I became distracted by the lovely goldfinch that landed on the new feeder; I ran into the house to fetch my binoculars so I could have a better look. At least I think it was a goldfinch: it was yellow and black, and looked a whole lot like the bird on the bag of seed I had bought—not that I really knew anything about birds. He was lovely. Or maybe it was a she. I couldn't tell. All I knew was that the sun was going down and it was getting cool.

I moved everything into the office only to realize that it was time to prepare for my evening coaching session. The following morning, I woke up with clear thoughts on what to write on the subject of guilt. I looked outside the window and, to my surprise, found that spring had gone; it was snowing. Great. I loved writing in winter. It was cozy and quiet and there were fewer distractions. I settled in the office with my coffee and muffin, got through my emails, opened up my text files and, for some reason, became obsessed with the document styles. I mended that situation too. Then I found myself staring at a plant next to my desk, an activity that appeared to be still far more important than writing. I had to laugh.

I love writing. But somehow, there was so much resistance to working on this material that I loved doing other things much more.

Even doing nothing was better than exploring the psychology of *A Course in Miracles,* and those who know me know that *doing nothing* never appears on my to-do list. So I got up, made a pot of tea—a final delaying tactic—and finally got down to work, but by then it was time to prepare another consultation. It would be a few more days before I sat down to work on this chapter, at which point, I decided to write this clever little aside, and when that was done, before looking sin, guilt and fear square in the eyes, I went off to bake a batch of muffins—cranberry and sunflower seed. If I was going to avoid writing, I might as well make it worth my while. Now that's resistance!

> Let me not forget myself is nothing, but my Self is all. (W-pII. 358.1:7)

Why the resistance? Quite simply, after five years of intensive study and work with the Course, the part of me that was identified with an experience of myself as a separate individual was no doubt growing wise to what continued study would eventually lead to; without a doubt, it was justifiably terrified. If this separate self was a false self, and I successfully uncovered and reconnected with my true Self, and this true Self was found to be a much better choice, then, in all likelihood the false self would simply be abandoned. I would no longer have any use for it, preferring to choose the true Self instead. In order to maintain its hold on my awareness and sustain its existence, the false self needed to find ways to prevent me from looking inside, for fear I might discover the truth. What is this truth that so frightens the false self that it would do whatever it takes to keep me from looking deeper?

The Insanity of Separation

> To learn this course requires willingness to question every value that you hold. Not one can be kept hidden and obscure but it will jeopardize your learning. No belief is neutral. Every one has the power to dictate each decision you make. For a

decision is a conclusion based on everything that you believe. (T-24.in.2:1–5)

In order to help us attain a direct experience of the truth, Jesus asks us to be willing to examine closely and question all of our beliefs, especially those we have taken for granted and accepted as truth all of our lives. In my first two to three years of work with the Course, in all honesty, I had no idea of what I was getting into. Since I have always considered myself to be a relatively open-minded person, I was ready to question every value that I held. However, it did not occur to me that should I find my deeply held beliefs and values to be untrue, I would have to let them go. When Jesus asks us to question every value, he means *every* value.

While modern psychology will shed light on human behaviour from within the perspective of the dream, being that it has evolved from the premise that we exist as separate individuals in a world that we believe to be real, that is the result of an act of creation by an external source, or God, it is not equipped to analyze the root cause of our seeming experience as individuals in a world that is not even real. To help us understand the true cause of our seemingly distinct bodily experiences, Jesus uses terminology of basic psychology, but he does so from a frame of reference that resides completely outside that of traditional psychology, from the premise that the world does not exist, and therefore our experience here in bodies can only be illusory.

Salvation is the recognition that the truth is true, and nothing else is true. This you have heard before, but may not yet accept both parts of it. Without the first, the second has no meaning. But without the second, is the first no longer true. Truth cannot have an opposite. This can not be too often said and thought about. For if what is not true is true as well as what is true, then part of truth is false. And truth has lost its meaning. Nothing but the truth is true, and what is false is false. (W-pI.152.3:1–9)

Jesus tells us that the truth is that only God is real and what is not of God is not real. Therefore, this world as we percieve it and experience it in our state of separation, is not of God, and cannot be real. At no point does the Course deviate from this statement of the truth. It is important to note that acceptance of this premise is essential to working with the Course, without which this teaching program will not work. Yet, we still have the problem of our experience that appears to tell us otherwise. In our pursuit of the truth about the origin of our existence, certain questions naturally arise. If our true condition is that we have never separated from our home in heaven with God, why then is this not our experience? Why do we have no recollection or awareness of this state? What's going on?

> The miracle establishes you dream a dream, and that its content is not true. This is a crucial step in dealing with illusions. No one is afraid of them when he perceives he made them up. The fear was held in place because he did not see that he was author of the dream, and not a figure in the dream. (T-28. II.7:1–4)

God–Heaven
(Oneness, Reality)

Not God–The World
(Duality, the Dream)

A return to the myth of separation can shed light on these questions. Keeping in mind that the mythology of the Course is a made-up story, the purpose of which is to help explain what we believe to be an actual condition, we begin at the beginning, with what is true, real and not mythical: God and His Creation. The Son of God, perfectly whole, always and forever at home with his Father, has a thought—one silly thought at which he forgets to laugh. What if I could be other than perfect oneness? In reality, this is an impossibility, because oneness would no longer be perfect. The Son of God can only entertain a thought of separation from outside the Mind of God, something that can occur only in a state of unreality, or in a dream, since nothing exists outside the Mind of God.

> Consciousness, the level of perception, was the first split introduced into the mind after the separation, making the mind a perceiver rather than a creator. Consciousness is correctly identified as the domain of the ego. The ego is a wrong-minded attempt to perceive yourself as you wish to be, rather than as you are. (T-3.IV.2:1–3)

By choosing to explore not-perfect-oneness, a state of duality emerges in the mind of the Son, thus establishing consciousness, or awareness of something outside oneself. There is an "I" and there is God, and one is distinct and separate from the other. Herein lies the birth of specialness, a very important item in the Course's agenda. All subsequent thoughts of specialness are rooted in this first thought that says, "I am distinct from my Father, I am special." The Son becomes aware of a state that is not real, since a thought of separation can only occur outside the Mind of God, and since nothing outside the Mind of God is real, the Son can never really *be* separate from the Father.

God–Oneness–Reality

Not God–Separated Self
Consciousness
(Thought of separation taken seriously)

Since the state of separation is not real, it cannot be sustained unless it is somehow made to appear real. The only way to make it appear real is to make what *is* real disappear. Our true condition at home in heaven, in a state of perfect oneness, fades from awareness and is replaced by a dream of separation. Where there are alternatives—oneness or separation—there is choice; where there is choice, perfect oneness appears to no longer exist. Having lost touch with his true condition, the Son of God now believes himself to exist outside the Mind of God and to be free of God's reign. In fact, he perceives himself as his own maker. Herein lies the root of all of our authority problems. Since God is out of the picture, it now appears as though I am my own creator.

From a psychological perspective, to believe in something that is not real can only be delusional, if not outright insane. Yet this is our belief, on top of which, we also believe that we are sane. From the moment we are born, we are groomed according to the rules and standards of our family, culture and times. As we grow up, in need of nurturing and support, we strive to have our needs met by adapting as best we can to the norms against which we are measured and the rules we are expected to obey. We go to school, socialize, hone a skill or two, grow up, get a job, find a mate and procreate. Most people will develop an adequate—or what we would regard as socially acceptable—way of handling themselves and the circumstances in their lives. In the eyes of the world, as we acquire effective coping mechanisms, we survive and even thrive.

Every community, every culture, every generation will have its share of members who have difficulty or are simply incapable of effectively developing acceptable coping mechanisms. These individuals are seen as misfits, outcasts or undesirables, and some are judged as the insane of our societies. However, looked at from the radical metaphysical perspective of *A Course in Miracles*, to believe that something that is not real—this world—can be made real can only be interpreted as insane. Since the Course also states that there is no hierarchy of illusions, to say that some people are "normal" while others are delusional is foolish.

From this perspective, the truth of the matter is that everyone is insane, and so our need to control, medicate and even ostracize the less sane members of our communities is a reflection of our wish to not be reminded of our own inner insanity. The majority of us are simply more adept at coping with the insanity of being apart from our true Selves, of believing in and maintaining a world that cannot be true and, most of all, of keeping the Love of God away. Since we would like to think that we are at least smart, and perhaps even clever, if our starting point is that we are all insane, this doesn't bode well for the hero of our dream—the seemingly separated self.

> God and His creations remain in surety, and therefore know that no miscreation exists.... I cannot unite your will with God's for you, but I can erase all misperceptions from your mind if you will bring it under my guidance. Only your misperceptions stand in your way. Without them your choice is certain. Sane perception induces sane choosing. I cannot choose for you, but I can help you make your own right choice. (T-3.IV.7:1, 7–11)

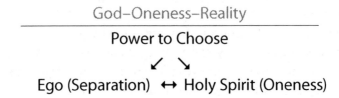

God–Oneness–Reality

Power to Choose

Ego (Separation) ↔ Holy Spirit (Oneness)

Now in a seeming state of separation, two ways of interpreting this apparent situation arise: on the one hand, there is the thought system of the ego, which is born of and reflects the original thought of separation, and, on the other hand, there is the thought system of the Holy Spirit, reflecting God's Answer to the tiny mad idea, which says that separation is not possible and in truth never happened. Only one of these alternatives can sustain the idea of separation, specialness and individuality; the other reflects the oneness of heaven.

Inherent in choice is judgment; the Son decides that it is better to be separated than to be one. Since separation cannot really occur, the reality of perfect oneness is never lost, it only fades from memory. God does not throw His Son out of the Kingdom as punishment for some misdeed or out of anger, as some religions would have us believe; rather, it is the Son who freely chooses to go down the road of separation. The Son now believes himself to be a separate, distinct individual. He is his own boss, he makes his own judgments and he has the power to make his own choices. While he has chosen with the ego, the memory of the Answer to the thought of separation, the Holy Spirit, is forgotten.

Innocence Lost

In order for the Son to continue to believe in a dream state and not return to his true state at home with God, there must be a powerfully compelling inner motivation, in fact, a darn good reason for him to choose a world of death over a life of unchanging wholeness, abundance and peace. Why would we choose to live in a dream? Why would anyone in their right mind reject the perfect oneness of God? Since the ego's existence is entirely dependent on the Son choosing it over the Holy Spirit, it must convince the Son to never, ever look inside. At any point, the Son of God can recognize the silliness of his separation fantasy, awaken from the dream and return to his true state of perfect oneness. But this would spell the end of the ego.

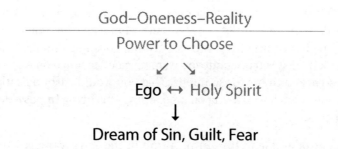

To prevent this from ever happening, the ego convinces the Son that his wonderful state of individuality came at a terrible price. In fact, to be an individual, separated self, he committed a horrible crime, a crime so heinous that it was deserving of the most severe punishment. With no voice other than the ego's to call on for help, the Son listens while the ego tells him this wild story of how he killed off God and now he's in big trouble. It makes sense. He is, after all, now experiencing separation. God is no longer here. God must be dead, and since there is no one else around, he must have done the killing. He's done a bad, bad thing.

> The Holy Spirit is one way of choosing. God did not leave His children comfortless, even though they chose to leave Him. The voice they put in their minds was not the Voice for His Will, for which the Holy Spirit speaks. (T-5.II.6:7–9)

Had the Son remembered to listen to the Holy Spirit, he would have been given an entirely different account; he would have been reminded that he is innocent, that he is still at Home with his Father, that he just had a silly thought and made the mistake of choosing to believe in something that was impossible in the first place. However, now believing that he has sinned, the Son begins to feel something new, and most disturbing—guilt. Now he's getting worried. If he has sinned, he's bound to be discovered and punished. The ego now has the Son where he wants him: trapped, with nowhere to turn and no memory of the truth.

> You think you are the home of evil, darkness and sin. You think if anyone could see the truth about you he would be repelled, recoiling from you as if from a poisonous snake. You think if what is true about you were revealed to you, you would be struck with horror so intense that you would rush to death by your own hand, living on after seeing this being impossible. (W-pI.93.1:1–3)

Sin, guilt and fear, the ammunition in the ego's war against the truth, are at the core of the psychology of *A Course in Miracles*, as they are the prime motivators for life in the dream. Sin is the thought that separation is a viable alternative to perfect oneness, that it is possible and that it has actually been achieved. It is the belief in the thought that says it is possible to accomplish the impossible, to separate from perfect oneness, to leave the Kingdom of Heaven. It is a murderous thought because separation from perfect oneness is impossible, since oneness would no longer be perfect.

Belief in Sin, Guilt and Fear

Of one thing you were sure: Of all the many causes you perceived as bringing pain and suffering to you, your guilt was not among them. (T-27.VII.7:4)

Guilt results when the thought of sin is taken seriously, rather than seen as a silly error. If I believe in my sinfulness, I must also believe in my guilt. Guilt is more difficult to deal with than error: it leaves a permanent scar, a stain that is impossible to remove, a scarlet letter that says you have sinned. Guilt cries out "Hide me! Deny me! Bury me so deep inside that I no longer appear to exist." An error, on the other hand, can easily be corrected and made to disappear. Until it has been seen for the error that it is, the deeply buried thought of guilt remains the primary driving force behind all of the thoughts, motivations and actions of the separated Son.

Fear results from the thought that punishment for the sin of having separated from God is inevitable. What we do not recognize is that it is the ego that is fearful for its own existence, and it is the ego that has in effect successfully projected its fear onto the sleeping Son. Everyone experiences fear on some level, even the meanest, cruellest person on the planet is afraid of something. And we love our fear! We feed it, nurture it, glorify it and then pretend we are

not fearful! We have enemies of earth, enemies of countries, terror-
ists, diseases, rush hour traffic, cyclones, hurricanes and, as if that
weren't enough, we invest billions of dollars in television shows and
movies designed to keep us huddled in our seats in terror or, for
those who prefer to read, well, there are enough books in the horror
genre to keep us awake nights for the rest of our lives. In fact, we
have made a very scary world. If God were to make a world for His
children, would He not make it a safe place?

Sin, guilt and fear establish for us—as bodies that are born, live
and ultimately die—the concept of time. Since at the core of our
beliefs about ourselves is the thought that we have sinned in the
past, we are now carrying a great burden of guilt and the fear of
inevitable punishment in some undetermined future. It is a belief
system with no way out, brilliantly designed to keep us constantly
running from the past, toward some unknown future. In essence,
it keeps us from the truth.

Denial, Repression and Projection

When it came time for me to think about and write this section,
as might be expected, more resistance arose. These are among the
most difficult teachings of the Course, because they clearly place
in the hands of the student the full responsibility for everything
in our lives—the good, the bad and the ugly. My profound fear of
examining this subject expressed itself as an urgent need to go
shopping at Costco, the premier item on my list being blueberries
for muffins. From the moment I sat at the computer that morning, I
had felt extreme tension in my back, so I justified the mid-morning
errand as an opportunity to give my back a rest. I was very much
aware of my resistance as I quickly went through my shopping list
and returned home, all the while forgiving myself for my resistance.
I also managed to think about my lesson for the day, "Forgiveness
offers everything I want" (W-pI.122), not because of any exceptional
diligence on my part, but rather because of the sense of guilt that
hovered menacingly in the back of my mind.

After grinding some fresh brown rice flour and laying out the ingredients for the muffins, however, I decided to stop. Guilt was rising to the surface, something I did not need to cultivate. In the Course, Jesus was asking me to look at my behaviour—in this case, my resistance to looking at the subject of projection. He was not asking me to judge myself for resisting. Just look. What I saw was resistance. Then I saw emerging guilt. Then I forgave myself. Then, I made a quick lunch and got down to the business of thinking about projection, its purpose and how it manifests in my life. Just look, without judgment. This was something I could do; I felt peaceful.

Admittedly, the thought that the Son has obtained autonomy and independence at the cost of murdering his Father is really not a very nice thought, but, Jesus tells us, it is at the core of our beliefs about ourselves. And because we believe it to be true, it is a problem for us and needs to be addressed. What the separated Son wants is to enjoy his experience of separateness, but if he is to survive—and at the very least be able to tolerate himself or, at best, love himself— he must do something with that horrible thought of sin and, even worse, the overwhelming guilt. He does not want to be responsible for all the bad stuff.

Now deeply entrenched in the ego's thought system of separation, the only thing the Son of God can do with a thought of this magnitude is to deny it ever happened, bury it deeply and throw away the key. He'll just pretend it never happened. This way of dealing with the problem works out quite well for the ego, since it ensures that the Son will never look inside: a brilliant defense strategy that also adds extra distance between the Son and his memory of his true place at home with God. This denial process is reflected in our automatic responses to accusations. The moment someone points an accusing finger at us, we almost instantly look for a scapegoat onto which we can project the guilt: "He made me do it. It's because of... I didn't know/see/hear. It's not my fault."

This solution cannot last long since, as psychology tells us, that which is repressed must eventually be expressed—or projected—and the Course tells us that the way in which the Son handles his thought of guilt is to project it outside himself. Again the ego, ever ready to find a way to stop any threat to its existence, adds a new twist to the plot: it makes God into the bad guy. God will no doubt find the Son, who will then surely be found guilty and deserving of punishment. That's just the way things work in the ego's insane world; if you are found guilty, you will be punished. Clearly insane, the Son doesn't stop to wonder how God, now dead, could possibly come back and judge him and find him guilty; he just takes this to be true. This God, made up by a separated mind, can only be like his maker: an angry, vengeful murderer. Herein lie the seeds of a great world religion in which its adherents are told to repent and atone for their sinful natures, cleanse themselves of the shadows of their evil ways and cast out the demons that corrupt their souls lest they be judged wanting and deserving of the fiercest punishment—eternal banishment from heaven.

The world was made as an attack on God. It symbolizes fear. And what is fear except love's absence? Thus the world was meant to be a place where God could enter not, and where His Son could be apart from Him. Here was perception born, for knowledge could not cause such insane thoughts. (W-pII.3.2:1–5)

The World: Not Such a Great Place After All!

When I finished writing these last few sections—a job that took many hours spread over a number of weeks—I needed to sit down. I know, I was already sitting. But work with me here, it's just a figure of speech. I needed to regroup, recentre, recap, reorient myself or do something to make sense of this head-spinning, mind-bending, upending and, admittedly, to a certain extent, distressing perspective on the origins of the universe and the meaning of existence. What Jesus is telling us is that there is nothing outside of the Mind of God; all of creation is still one with God, in heaven. This means that anything that appears to be outside the Mind of God is not real, and so this world, this entire universe, is an illusion. Furthermore, what appears to happen outside is a picture of what has been projected from the mind of the Son, an outside picture of a very troubling condition: the condition being the Son's belief in his sinfulness, the guilt over this thought and the resulting fear of punishment, which all lead to the need to get rid of the whole nasty mess.

Contrary to our age-old beliefs about God having created the universe and all things in it and being pleased with His work, Jesus tells us that the real source of the world is the Son's belief in his guilt. This guilt causes so much fear that a world had to be projected outside the Son's mind. From this perspective, there is nothing terribly glorious or even redeeming about this world that we hold so dear. And since there is no hierarchy of illusions, the Course tells us, everything that we see outside is a picture of what is going on inside. All of it: the good with the bad, even the most perfect summer day. As long as we, as splintered off parts of the one Son, continue to believe in the ego's story of our sinfulness, we need a world onto which we can project the guilt. Take away the guilt, and the need for the world disappears. It is guilt that keeps us in the desert; if we could but realize that there is no guilt, the desert would disappear.

Suffering Not Required

> I do not want you to allow any fear to enter into the thought system toward which I am guiding you. I do not call for martyrs but for teachers. No one is punished for sins, and the Sons of God are not sinners. Any concept of punishment involves the projection of blame, and reinforces the idea that blame is justified. (T-6.I.16:2–5)

I was raised Catholic. When I was young, I very much enjoyed reading the lives of the Christian mystics. However, there was one element in the teachings of the Church that didn't sit well with me: it was the idea that suffering was a good thing, even a very holy and necessary thing. Not a big fan of suffering, I always believed that I would never make it to the ranks of the holy and most definitely not to sainthood. Fortunately, Jesus does not expect us, nor does he ask us, to suffer. Despite the fact that, with my growing understanding of the Course, the outlook for life in the world appeared bleaker than ever, I must admit that I was pleased that suffering was not going to be a condition for awakening from the dream.

I sometimes hear people describe their spiritual journeys as an evolutionary process of sorts in which certain skills and aptitudes were developed, a required journey, one that was necessary to get them to where they are now and just as necessary to get to where they want to go. While, to a point, this is true in the world in which we believe ourselves to be, lack of progress, challenges, obstacles and struggles should not be taken as requirements to learning the lessons of *A Course in Miracles*. While the belief that trials and tribulations are imposed on us by some higher intelligence for our own learning is integral to some spiritual thought systems, it is clearly not consistent with the teachings of the Course. Our having fallen asleep and our dream experience are the consequences of our having chosen to believe that it is possible to be other than perfectly whole, at home with God. This is our choice. While the life journey that we experience serves the purposes of this choice, the Course teaches that it can just as easily serve the purposes of a journey of awakening.

Some will try to spiritualize their life dramas, saying that they needed to experience such-and-such a tragedy in order to stop and reconsider their beliefs or their bad choices. Some will go so far as to thank God for sending them a wake-up call. Though maybe the stuff of a great movie of the week or best-selling novel, suffering of any kind was never inflicted on us by God for the purpose of making us turn toward Him for salvation. Only a cruel and demented father could wish that for his children.

As a good Catholic, I was taught to be humble before the Glory of God and his Creation, which included heaven and earth and all things therein. Repeatedly, we were told that we are small, insignificant nothings compared to God, plus, we are sinful and guilty and should pray for forgiveness. Hopefully, we prayed, we had not offended God too much and, if we obeyed the laws of the Church, we might be lucky enough to secure a place in heaven for ourselves when we die. Pass the collection plate please.[1] From this perspective, to say that *we* made up the world and all things in it, as the Course says, would be deemed arrogance of heretical proportions.

Jesus tells us that quite the opposite is true. To believe that God could create anything that is less than perfect is arrogant. To bow down before this supposedly God-created imperfect world is not humility, but arrogance. True humility would accept that we are as God created us, spirit, whole, safe and at one with all Creation. To think otherwise is arrogance. In truth, we are responsible for the world we see and how we choose to see it. We set up the circumstances of our lives to suffer grief, loss, sorrow and pain in order to make separation real. When something "happens to me," it proves that there is a "me." Furthermore, what is happening appears to be coming from outside of me and is therefore not my fault. I am, in effect, the victim of circumstances that are outside my control. Poor me.

If a tragic life event should turn our attention inwards, it is not because God is sending us a message, it is because it has struck a chord with our deeply buried memory of the truth. Besides, if God put something "out there" for any reason whatsoever, it would make "out there" real, which is contrary to what the Course teaches. God did not put suffering in our lives in order for us to turn "inwards," since there is no outward from which to turn; there is only one place, perfect oneness.

> Is it not strange that you believe to think you made the world you see is arrogance? God made it not. Of this you can be sure. What can He know of the ephemeral, the sinful and the guilty, the afraid, the suffering and lonely, and the mind that lives within a body that must die? You but accuse Him of insanity, to think He made a world where such things seem to have reality. He is not mad. Yet only madness makes a world like this.

---

1. For those unfamiliar with the Catholic Mass, following the sermon, a plate is passed around to collect donations for the parish.

To think that God made chaos, contradicts His Will, invented opposites to truth, and suffers death to triumph over life; all this is arrogance. Humility would see at once these things are not of Him. And can you see what God created not? To think you can is merely to believe you can perceive what God willed not to be. And what could be more arrogant than this?

Today we practice true humility, abandoning the false pretense by which the ego seeks to prove it arrogant. Only the ego can be arrogant. But truth is humble in acknowledging its mightiness, its changelessness and its eternal wholeness, all-encompassing, God's perfect gift to His beloved Son. We lay aside the arrogance which says that we are sinners, guilty and afraid, ashamed of what we are; and lift our hearts in true humility instead to Him Who has created us immaculate, like to Himself in power and in love. (W-pI.152.6–7; 9)

Mirror, Mirror...

Though I do not have a background in psychology, I had on many occasions observed the process of projection at work, mostly in other people (not in myself, of course). As an autonomous, self-reliant, highly functional individual, I had never considered myself to have much use for projection, so this aspect of the Course's teaching did not come easily for me. I had to think really hard about the fact that Jesus tells us flatly that *everything* outside the Mind of God is a projection and so everything I see outside is really a picture of what is going on inside my mind.

I had been studying the Course for four years when my mother moved in with me—the single event that would cause me to get very, very serious with my Course studies. It was a sunny Sunday morning in late May, and in my dream I had made weekends in the garden important. In the springtime, weather permitting, I would be happily working in the garden, what I affectionately called my little piece of heaven. I had already sacrificed the first half of that lovely weekend in the basement bottling wine with my mom.

With the sun shining brightly, naturally I was eager to get out of the basement and into the garden. There was evidently a hierarchy among my illusions!

My mom is a bit obsessive about cleaning. Keeping house is what she had always done, and it is something she does well. After answering my emails, I joined her in the basement to see if she was ready to plant some flowers. Excitedly, she called me over to show me how she had found a way to remove the stains from the primary fermenters, the large white plastic pails used for winemaking. She was quite pleased with her discovery, but, in my mind, the pails were stained, not dirty, and quite acceptable for doing the job they were designed to do. A few grape stains would not affect the quality of the wine. To me, this was not an efficient use of time. The sun was shining and flowers awaited planting. Spending another half day in the basement was certainly not a welcome option. Despite the fact that cleaning the pails was not unimportant to my mom, and despite having pledged to be kind, I needed to get outside. Mumbling something about the stains not being a priority, and not wanting to spend the day scrubbing the pails, I left the basement and went out into the garden.

While in the garden, I got to thinking about my mom's obsession with cleanliness, a habit that was beginning to fray my nerves. Looked at from the perspective of the Course, it appeared as a symbol of an unconscious need to scrub out the blemish of sin. On a number of occasions, I could have pointed out that she was not logical in her obsession with cleanliness, given her preference for public transportation over the car. I often imagined the germs and other nasty unmentionables accumulating on the railings that she had to grip while enjoying her bus rides downtown. But I never brought up my objections; I just let her do her thing.

No doubt prompted by feelings of guilt, it occurred to me that I could have been kinder to my mom. I could have said how wonderful it was that she had found a way to remove the stains from the fermenters, that they looked just like new, but I think I was afraid she would expect me to stay downstairs to scrub the pails with her. I had other plans that day. My urgent priority was to cut the branches that had grown over my flower beds from the neighbour's unkempt yard in the back. While my mom was cleaning pails in the basement, I was happily cutting, pruning and uprooting anything that was in the way of my prized garden.

Well, mostly happily. All the while, I continued to go over the situation in my mind, trying to zero in on what didn't feel quite right, until it hit me. It seems that we all have our obsessions, and the real reason my mom's obsession with cleaning irked me was that it reflected back my own generally very obsessive nature, which in this case found expression in an urgent need to get rid of the offending branches from the neighbour's yard. Maintaining my space and protecting the boundaries of my property by removing the invading branches was a symbol of my desire to protect my separateness, but by not sharing in my mom's pleasure, I had also kept love away, another subtle ploy of the ego to maintain separation.

Guilty as Charged

When I first began to study the Course, I didn't see the sin, let alone the guilt. Other than a vague sense of uneasiness about taking money from clients, as though, deep down, I believed that what I did had no monetary value, I didn't see the guilt. Even as I began to work with the Course, I thought I could get by without looking at guilt. But as a Course student, I was being asked to pay attention. If I wanted to awaken from the dream, I would necessarily have to look inside and acknowledge my belief in my sinful nature before I could actually embrace my innocence.

As a good Catholic girl, I was much more in touch with my fear, always careful to obey the rules of the Church and avoid sin as much as possible. Evidently, the guilt was cleverly camouflaged by good behaviour. Generally being a good person, I was oblivious to the thought of sin, and so there was no outward evidence of guilt, nor of any cause for guilt. Until, of course, I began to scratch beneath the surface. It took nearly four years of study and work with the Course before I could begin to consider that there might be a little guilt hidden deep down inside. But then, once I became aware of it, it became a Pandora's box: I began to see it everywhere. It didn't matter what I did or did not do, there was guilt. I bought a television and felt guilty; even though I justified the purchase by reminding myself that I had saved up the money for several months, I still felt guilty. Then I bought a DVD player and converter to match the technology of the new television, of course, adding more guilt. If I attended an event, whether for family or business, that I did not really feel like attending, I felt guilty; if I didn't go, I felt guilty. It seemed that it didn't matter what I did or did not do, the result was guilt.

The real eye-opener came when I was given a ticket for a traffic violation. It was a lovely day, and I had set aside a few hours in the middle of the week to take my mom shopping and run a few errands. I wasn't driving fast, barely doing the speed limit at 40 kilometres per hour, but I did my usual time-saving roll through in second gear at a stop sign. In a split second, I heard the siren burst and saw the police cruiser pull out of the intersection perpendicular to where I had barely rolled through my stop. "I guess you didn't like my stop," I said to the young female officer, who appeared to take her job extremely seriously. She didn't smile as she took my papers and wrote out the ticket. As I drove away, my mom opened the ticket and exclaimed with horror when she saw the one-hundred-and-fifty-four-dollar fine.

I had to laugh when I remembered my lesson for the day, "I am under no laws but God's" (W-pI.76). As best I could, not wanting to ruin an otherwise lovely outing, I decided to forget about the nasty little contravention, and effectively submerged the memory of the experience. It was only the following day, when I wrote out my cheque and filled out the form—on which I checked off the "Guilty" box, then noticed the three demerit points—that the whole thing really hit me. It wasn't so much the hundred and fifty-four dollars—I would survive—it was more the admission of guilt, the demerit points that would stay with me for two years and, of course, the loss of my lifelong unblemished record. The unpleasant memory of this intimate tête-à-tête with guilt stayed with me for months.

The Course says that "I am never upset for the reason I think" (W.pI.5). I was upset. It appeared as though I was upset for getting a traffic ticket, but I was really upset for having been found guilty, and for my record having become permanently tarnished. The next time I took the car out for a drive, I made sure to come to a full stop. No more starting in second gear. While it would take a couple of months to train myself out of my bad driving habit, this little encounter caused me to do a whole lot of thinking. In fact, my intense feeling of upset revealed a lot of elements at play. I was not only angry about my tarnished record, I hated the ambitious little police officer for her eagerness in playing out her authority role, clearly a symbol of the ultimate authority, God, who can pull the plug on my guilty separated self at any time He so desires.

I also thought about my quirky driving habit. It was a shortcut and, given my impatient nature, allowed me to get through my intersections faster. But why the rush? This would not have happened had I simply followed the road regulations and come to a full stop. No one made full stops in this town; all those other drivers out there were as guilty as I was. It seemed that I was always in a hurry to get to one valueless place or another. While I was in a hurry, I was not thinking about my wish to go Home, my true goal; I was too busy rushing around in the dream. Then I thought, if I come to a full stop, it will take more time for me to start up again, and I was afraid that the driver behind me would become impatient, blast his horn, smash into my bumper, yell at me. And, there it was—I was projecting my own impatience onto other drivers. It was my dream, my projection, my fear, my guilt. What a silly dream!

Only Two Emotions

> You have but two emotions, and one you made and one was given you. Each is a way of seeing, and different worlds arise from their different sights.

... The course does not aim at teaching the meaning of love, for that is beyond what can be taught. It does aim, however, at removing the blocks to the awareness of love's presence, which is your natural inheritance. (T-13.V.10:1–2; T-in.1:6–7)

The Course tells us that there are only two emotions: love and fear. The first arises naturally from the knowledge that only the changeless perfect oneness of God exists. The second is born of the belief in the mistaken thought that says that separation from God is possible, that it has occurred and that it was obtained at a very dear price. The first is real; the second is made up and therefore unreal. All other emotions find their basis in either love or fear.

Although you are one Self, you experience yourself as two; as both good and evil, loving and hating, mind and body. This sense of being split into opposites induces feelings of acute and constant conflict, and leads to frantic attempts to reconcile the contradictory aspects of this self-perception. (W-pI.96.1:1–2)

While we maintain the thought that separation from perfect oneness is possible—a thought that can only lead to feelings of guilt, fear, grief and loss—deep in our hearts, what we really seek is the love that never fails, the love we denied and rejected when we chose separation over the oneness of God. Beneath every need, every desire, every wish, every compulsion, every motivation lies our longing for the Love of God, for which the loves of this world are but a pale and, ultimately, unsatisfactory substitute. Everything we do in the world is either an attempt to find and recapture this love, or the fulfillment of a wish to keep love away. Since the separation never happened and perfect love remains intact, to push love away reflects a desire to hold on to the dream of separation a little while longer. The pain and suffering we endure is the price we pay for choosing illusion over truth, separation over oneness.

Born out of the thought of separation, fear is the emotion that stands between us and the Love of God. It is the consequence of having chosen against love and serves as the basic motivation for the thought system of the ego. It says that there is something really horrible hidden deep inside and we must work very hard at protecting ourselves from the very real threats to our existence. One only has to look at the world we made, what Ken Wapnick calls "a maladaptive solution to a non-existent problem," filled with dangers and never-ending threats to our survival. Driven by our need to keep guilt deeply buried, fear is the basis for all other emotions, including anger, impatience, frustration, sadness and, in particular, hatred. When someone even just hints at our guilt, watch how quickly we jump up in anger and defensiveness. As long as we believe ourselves to be bodies, a state that is unnatural, we must put up defences against threats of attack. We are vulnerable, fearful, anxious. Separation from wholeness and oneness leads to a state of lack and scarcity, which compels us to compensate by constantly trying to fill the emptiness with the love and admiration of other bodies, material and intellectual acquisitions—an emptiness that can never be filled, since the things of this world are not real.

The dream was not made by God; it is completely foreign to God. Since God's Love is all-encompassing and what He creates must be like Himself, what He did not create—the world and all things in it and of it—cannot be like Him and therefore must be a place that is not real. Where God is not, love cannot enter; in its place, there must be love's opposite, fear. Since only the Love of God is real, fear must be unreal. Since what is of God is perfectly whole and can never be what it is not, fear must hide our inner call for love. Any emotion that does not reflect oneness, shared interests or kindness is a call for love, for only love is true.

Since the Love of God is a love that extends from perfect oneness, it can never be fully experienced as long as we cling to a belief in separation and separate interests. What we experience as love in this world cannot be the Love of God. The loves, the likes, the joys, the happiness, the passions, the cherished things of this world do not last. Our worldly loves are capricious, conditional, vulnerable and susceptible to change, and can quickly be turned to hate. God's Love is unchanging, boundless, constant and all-inclusive. The love of which Jesus speaks is a love that is beyond this world. Therefore, it is beyond anything that we could ever fully understand as bodies in a world. It is the love that is known when oneness is experienced.

> Loudly the ego tells you not to look inward, for if you do your eyes will light on sin, and God will strike you blind. This you believe, and so you do not look. Yet this is not the ego's hidden fear, nor yours who serve it. Loudly indeed the ego claims it is; too loudly and too often. For underneath this constant shout and frantic proclamation, the ego is not certain it is so. Beneath your fear to look within because of sin is yet another fear, and one which makes the ego tremble.
> What if you looked within and saw no sin? This "fearful" question is one the ego never asks. And you who ask it now are threatening the ego's whole defensive system too seriously for it to bother to pretend it is your friend. (T-21.IV.2:3–8; 3:1–3)

The fear of being found guilty covers the ego's secret fear that we, as split-off parts of the one Son, might look deeper, that we might remember that the whole idea of separation is a silly mistake, an impossibility, and that we might then choose the peace that comes from accepting our true condition, our oneness with our Father. Our greatest fear is that we might realize that we are sinless, there-fore guiltless, that we are as God created us, that we are loved, truly, a realization that would mark the end of our need to maintain our illusory state of separateness.

J and the Drunken Sailor

When I was young, struggling to make my place in the world, to be loved and to survive, I learned that being quiet was better than expressing my emotions. So I shut up and put up. I learned that being good, obeying the rules, doing as I was told would get me what I needed. So I became a good girl—an easy, docile child, my mother would say with a certain pride. I observed that polite, caring, thoughtful and kind grown-ups were more likely to be appreci-ated and accepted than mean, cruel, loud and obnoxious ones, so I grew up to be a nice grown-up. Throughout my life, people have remarked on my calm demeanor, some have even said that they felt good being in my presence. Sometimes I would respond jokingly that it was all on the surface. Though I did not quite understand why, I sensed that deep down, there lurked storms of overwhelming dread and anger. For fear of unleashing these storms, I became very adept at maintaining an appearance of superficial calm and peace. That is, until I became a student of *A Course in Miracles*, at which time, all hell broke loose as the gates to the calm exterior burst open and dark, nasty emotions slithered uninvited to the surface.

In the Course, Jesus describes his students as smiling more frequently, as having a serene forehead and quiet eyes and being more peaceful. Three years into my Course studies, it seemed that as much as I wanted some of those nice experiences, I was headed in the opposite direction and I wasn't smiling about it. My natural propensity to impatience grew more evident, especially with the most insignificant things, like my computer, unsolicited emails or road traffic. One of my computer programs would freeze up, I'd snap and the most unladylike language would appear in my mind. It was as though an angry drunken sailor had taken hostage of my otherwise polite mind. I also started to resent being with people, preferring to be on my own. Then I started to hate people, randomly. There didn't seem to be a pattern; anyone was a likely candidate for the projection of my hatred. Sometimes I felt as though I hated everybody. Having had decades of experience with burying my feelings, I doubt that my clients or anyone noticed the colourful evolution of my spiritual journey, but I noticed it, and even I might have blushed a few times.

Since all of these feelings could not remain buried forever, they needed to be projected onto something. At first, they found convenient targets in the unwitting spiritual communities—especially those that did not subscribe to *A Course in Miracles*, which my ego had made into something very important in my life. My resentment, hatred and annoyance then found ideal targets in the "bliss ninny" *Course in Miracles* community of teachers and students who were happily expounding the joyful message of the Course. In fact, I resented that others seemed so happy, joyful, kind and peaceful while I wasn't experiencing any of those nice feelings on my Course journey. Clearly, I was not becoming a happy learner. In counterpoint to the bliss ninnies, I had in fact become a full-blown "bitch ninny." There was no way in Hades that my ego-driven self was going to allow true joy into my life, let alone peace, kindness and love. My ego-identified self, no doubt disturbed by my having stirred the illusory pot of separation through my work with the Course, had taken hold of the reins and was deriving a particularly perverse pleasure from my dreadfully dark disposition.

Not wanting to remain a bitch ninny forever, I remembered to take Jesus' hand. I knew that he would not judge me; he was, after all, once a fisherman and must have had a few sailor friends. I knew that I shouldn't judge myself either. It was clear that my resentments and impatience masked the fear of the love that lay just beyond the wall of separation, the Love of God that is our natural inheritance, the love that would naturally extend to all my brothers, no matter what seemed to be occurring in the dream. Fortunately, Jesus does not ask us to modify our behaviour or our feelings, he does not ask us to be kind, peaceful or loving. He says only that these are qualities that will naturally develop, over time, with regular practice of the Course's teachings. This I saw as a very good thing; otherwise, *A Course in Miracles* would not have been for me. I could not pretend to love; if I could, I would not have been in touch with the anger, the hatred and the fear that blocked the way to the awareness of the presence of the Love of God. It would be a long journey, but it was a journey I would not turn down for anything in the universe. It was the journey out of the desert.

> The outcome of the lesson that God's Son is guiltless is a world in which there is no fear, and everything is lit with hope and sparkles with a gentle friendliness. (T-31.I.8:1)

Chapter 6

A TALE OF TWO MINDS

You who have tried to learn what you do not want should take heart, for although the curriculum you set yourself is depressing indeed, it is merely ridiculous if you look at it. Is it possible that the way to achieve a goal is not to attain it? Resign now as your own teacher. This resignation will not lead to depression. It is merely the result of an honest appraisal of what you have taught yourself, and of the learning outcomes that have resulted. Under the proper learning conditions, which you can neither provide nor understand, you will become an excellent learner and an excellent teacher. (T-12.V.8:1–6)

I've Lost My Mind!

WHY WOULD ANYONE IN their right mind choose anything but perfect peace? Why would anyone in their right mind fear the Love of God? Why would anyone in their right mind choose a life of struggle, suffering and death instead of a life of perfect wholeness, abundance and peace? The only reasonable explanation for this state of affairs is that I am not in my right mind. If I am not in my right mind, I must be in my wrong mind, which means that I must have another mind. If I have another mind, where is it? Why am I not in touch with it? How do I get back to it? Who is it that decides which mind I will choose? If I am responsible for having chosen a life devoid of God, death over life, strife over peace, I need to fire myself as my own boss, for I certainly am not terribly wise, in fact, I must be insane.

This line of questioning, though seemingly logical, had me in trouble right from the start, for it assumed that the "I" who was asking the questions might actually have the answers. How could "I" know anything about a part of my mind of which "I" had no knowledge? Of course, I wanted peace. Of course, I had a mind. And, of course, I made decisions, constantly. I had successfully harnessed the power of my mind to learn complex tasks and to survive and even thrive in a very complicated world. In fact, I considered myself to be relatively intelligent, somewhat clever and certainly resourceful enough to deal with most anything that life had to offer. Yet, for some reason, my decisions did not always lead to peace—at least, not the peace for which I longed, the quiet peace of a lasting kind, the peace of God. If I truly wanted that peace, why then did I not consistently make peaceful choices? Many of the decisions I made seemed to come automatically, almost without thinking. In fact, in my mind, decisions were constantly being made, not necessarily with my conscious approval and not always with peaceful outcomes. Was there a part of my mind of which I was unaware?

> You may believe that you are responsible for what you do, but not for what you think. The truth is that you are responsible for what you think, because it is only at this level that you can exercise choice. What you do comes from what you think.... You must change your mind, not your behavior, and this is a matter of willingness. You do not need guidance except at the mind level. (T-2.VI.2:5–7; 3:4–5)

Jesus tells us that the truth is that God is, and that's it. Then we cease to speak. But here I was, still yammering on, laa, laa, laa ... besides which, by the looks of it, I was beginning to think that I might actually be insane—not from the perspective of the world, but from the perspective of the metaphysics of the Course—insane meaning "not sane," as in making choices that lead to results that were contrary to my desire, such as attracting "not peace" instead of peace. Since I had clearly established that my goal is to awaken from the dream and return to my true home with God and that peace was a condition for the attainment of that goal, sooner or later, I would have to connect with that choice point in my mind and sort things out, once and for all. Despite my fervent and diligent study of *A Course in Miracles*, as a decidedly "non-holy" person, that choice point seemed light years away, well beyond the reach of my perceptual brain, that aspect of my mind with which I pondered these convoluted metaphysical questions. Without a clear understanding of how my mind worked, I remained trapped in the darkness of my dream oasis, unable to see the light beyond. Where was that mind with the power to make a different choice? How could I get in touch with a mind that was buried so deep that I was completely unaware of its existence? And besides, why was this mind so deeply hidden from my awareness?

> Ask not the sparrow how the eagle soars, for those with little wings have not accepted for themselves the power to share with you.... Who would attempt to fly with the tiny wings of a sparrow when the mighty power of an eagle has been given him? (T-20.IV.4:7; M-4.I.2:2)

Five years into my studies, I was familiar enough with the teachings of *A Course in Miracles* to know that it addresses all these questions—and so many more—but it was equally clear that the answers frightened me, as shown when it came time to work on this chapter. As with the previous chapter, I must admit that I encountered a little resistance—even a lot of resistance. As a first clue, to ensure that I would not delve into the dark corners of my mind any sooner than necessary, I found myself booking consultations on Fridays, my writing day, technically blocked off for the six-month period I had set aside to finish the first draft of this book.

On one of those Friday mornings, at that quiet moment when the mind shifts from the sleeping dream to the waking dream, that moment of pure stillness and clarity that quickly slips from awareness once the brain hits the daily to-do list, I had the very clear message that I should go shopping for a digital recording device to replace my antiquated microcassette recorder. I could then record my thoughts and upload my notes directly into my computer using my voice recognition program, saving my arms, shoulders and back from undue wear. It sounded like a good idea, and it would facilitate my writing. With that thought in mind, I got up, dressed, had a quick coffee and muffin, then headed out to the store.

It was mid-May, time to clean up the garden and choose the summer's plantings, and since my freezer was well-stocked with muffins,[1] between consultations and work, there were plenty of new distractions to get in my way of writing. I don't quite know how this happened, but instead of landing at the electronics store, I ended up in the opposite direction, at the nursery, shopping for geraniums, begonias and impatiens—the flower, that is, not my personality flaw. I even let myself be tempted into buying a rather expensive new hybrid of echinacea called Tomato Soup. It wasn't until I had returned home that it occurred to me that I had forgotten completely about my new writing tool.

I don't know if it was my study and practice of the Course that was slowing me down, perhaps mellowing me out, but, to my surprise, I found myself doing a little birdwatching between consults. The pair of goldfinches were now a family, so it was common to see three of them at the feeder. One of them sang for me—well, probably for its mate, but I pretended it was for me—a long, mournful, question mark of a song. The cardinals brought the first of their litter too, or whatever it is that bird babies are called, and I watched the male fill his mouth with sunflower seeds, which he then brought to the female. This was their mating ritual. Interestingly, he fed himself before he fed either his mate or junior; he was a true survivor. I think I even saw a pair of sparrows picking up fallen seeds in the flower bed below, not Jesus' favourite bird, I know, but there were no eagles in my backyard. I later learned that my fine feathered friends were not sparrows but house finches. I didn't think Jesus

---

1. For the resistant reader desiring a delicious distraction, my marvellous muffin recipe can be found at the end of this book.

would have been any more impressed with the finches: they still were not eagles.[2]

Of Choice and Consequences

As I did want to fly with the wings of the eagle, there was no choice but to examine why I chose with the sparrow. I smiled at my resistance, somewhat encouraged by the thought that it indicated I might be touching close to home; perhaps this was a sign of progress. Since Jesus knew the answer to my questions and, more importantly, knew the way home, I set aside my fear of uncovering what lay hidden in the dark recesses of my mind and studied closely what he had to say on the matter. Since the best place to start is always at the beginning, it was necessary to examine once again how this entire mind mess began in the first place, which meant one more round with the myth of separation and the increasingly tiresome trio of sin, guilt and fear!

> Ideas leave not their source, and their effects but seem to be apart from them. Ideas are of the mind. What is projected out, and seems to be external to the mind, is not outside at all, but an effect of what is in, and has not left its source. (T-26. VII.4:7–9)

The Course explains quite simply that our starting point is a thought in the mind of the Son of God who wonders in passing what it might be like to be separate from perfect oneness, something that could never be real, since perfect oneness would not be perfect. Essential to the Course's teaching is the principle that says ideas do not leave their source. Since no thought exists outside the Mind of God, a thought of separation cannot lead to anything outside the Mind of God that is real, let alone a physical universe filled with

---

2. The reader familiar with my work with numerology may find it amusing to note that this section, and the other on resistance in the previous chapter were written in a number 3 Personal Month, the 3 being associated with distractions, entertainment, creativity and joie de vivre. This distracting footnote was written on a 3 Personal Day.

billions of worlds, bodies and things. The thought of separation remains in the mind of the Son. This is our starting point—one thought in the mind of the Son, who remains always in the Mind of God, as His Creation. One silly impossible thought that disappeared as soon as it seemed to arise back into the nothingness from which it came and that's the end of that!

God–Oneness–Reality

Ability to Choose: The Decision Maker

As we know, the Son, attracted to the idea of existence outside of the Mind of God, decides to take the thought of separation seriously. He considers his options: perfect oneness or individuality. Perfect oneness sounds boring; individuality sounds exciting and even looks very promising. Hmm… he ponders. Feeling brave and adventurous, he makes a choice: he fancies being a separate individual. The part of the mind in which this choice is made is what Ken Wapnick appropriately calls the *decision maker*. This is where the original error was made, a part of the mind that is now completely veiled from our awareness, but also the part of the mind with which we must become reacquainted if we are to fly with the wings of the eagle.

Knowing this, and since I sincerely wished to experience the peace of God so I could eventually return home, why didn't I simply go to that decision-making place in my mind and choose oneness right then, right there? Since I seem to always be in a hurry to get to wherever it is I think I need to be, why not choose the quick option, get it over with, just switch to the right mind? If it is what would lead to an experience of peace, wouldn't that be the smart thing to do? It appears that I may not have been as ready to go home as I thought. There remained a couple of very good reasons why I did not simply decide to go home and be done with the whole business of life in a body.

<u>God–Oneness–Reality</u>

The Decision Maker

↙ ↘

Ego (Separation) ↔ Holy Spirit (Oneness)

As already seen, when the Son of God chose to pursue the thought of separation, two distinct thought systems emerged: the thought system of the ego that says separation is possible and has actually occurred, and its alternative, the thought system of the Holy Spirit, the memory of the truth, that says nothing happened and perfect oneness remains unharmed, intact and unchanged. Since the two cannot coexist, once the Son chose with the ego, the thought system of oneness faded into the background and he forgot that he once had another option. Oneness does not disappear, nor is it ever destroyed; it simply remains where it always was. However, as long as the Son pursues the thought of separation, it remains out of awareness.

> Few appreciate the real power of the mind, and no one remains fully aware of it all the time.... The mind is very powerful, and never loses its creative force. It never sleeps. Every instant it is creating. It is hard to recognize that thought and belief combine into a power surge that can literally move mountains. It appears at first glance that to believe such power about yourself is arrogant, but that is not the real reason you do not believe it. You prefer to believe that your thoughts cannot exert real influence because you are actually afraid of them. This may allay awareness of the guilt, but at the cost of perceiving the mind as impotent. If you believe that what you think is ineffectual you may cease to be afraid of it, but you are hardly likely to respect it. There are no idle thoughts. All thinking produces form at some level. (T-2.VI.9:3, 5–14)

A funny thing happens when thoughts are expressed—they have consequences, and that first thought of separation appears to have had very real consequences. Choosing implies that there is more than one thing from which to choose, an impossibility in the Mind of God, which can express only what is true: perfect oneness. There are no choices to be made in perfect wholeness, nothing to choose with, for, between or against. So the only possible consequence for such a thought is of no consequence, unless one takes the choosing seriously, which, as we know, is what appears to have happened. Fortunately, the Course makes it very clear that just because the Son chooses to take the thought of separation seriously—the consequence of which is a world of duality—it does not make separation real.

We make choices all the time, in fact, freedom of choice has become almost a basic human right. We pride ourselves in the abundance of options and alternatives we have in all areas of life in a world of ever-increasing possibilities, and we see this as a good thing, interpreting it as progress. We cherish choice. Who would want to eat in a restaurant with only one item on the menu? We want everyone in the world to share in the same unlimited opportunities.

But this is not the level at which Jesus is asking us to consider our choices. If it were, he would be just as insane as the rest of us, who believe in the reality of this world. Besides that, if we had to sort through all the possible choices in this world in order to get to the truth, there would be no hope, for there would be no end to it. No matter how many choices we have—and make—in the world, they remain a pale substitute for the truly powerful choice that lies within. In fact, the Course makes it quite simple and states that there are only two real choices: truth or illusion.

Throughout the Course, Jesus attempts to have us turn our attention inwards, to that place in the mind, where we could make a different choice. However, try as he might, he has a very tough job on his hands, since this place in our minds where we can choose between Reality and the dream, is no longer in our awareness. Interestingly, it is at a time in our lives when we are most likely to question our origins—the later years—that many of us will experience the common ailment of memory loss. This looks very much like a cleverly conceived survival mechanism of the ego, designed to ensure that we do not stop and look inside. How can we turn inwards when we have forgotten that there is an inward?

> The choice to judge rather than to know is the cause of the loss of peace.... Judgment always involves rejection. It never emphasizes only the positive aspects of what is judged, whether in you or in others. What has been perceived and rejected, or judged and found wanting, remains in your mind because it has been perceived. (T-3.VI.2:1, 4–6)

An essential feature of this choosing privilege is judgment; the Son has judged that to be separate from perfect oneness is more desirable than to remain united with God in Heaven. Judging means that one thing is better than another, which means that all is not the same, all is no longer one, something that can only occur in a mind that is born of separation. In perfect oneness, since there is only sameness, judgment cannot occur. All thoughts of judgment reinforce differences. Differences are essential to maintaining the illusion of separation; separation keeps us from the knowledge that we are one with God. Differences also keep love away, since love can only be experienced in oneness. As long as there is something outside deserving of our judgment, there is an outside, there is a separated self that is different from what has been deemed deserving of our judgment. From the perspective of the separated self, judgment is an essential function; from the perspective of a whole Self, judgment is non-existent.

I don't think I have ever met anyone who was not at least a little bit sensitive to criticism, the reason now being made quite clear. Since what we see outside is a picture of the beliefs we harbour inside, when we witness judgment we are really recognizing, though unconsciously, a reflection of that initial judgment in which we, as the Son of God, decided that separation was better than the perfect oneness of God. This thought stirs up our old friend guilt; so feeling judged, a form of attack, we become defensive and may even attack back. We rid ourselves of our guilt by finding fault in others—essentially, by judging them. That way, it appears as though they are guilty and we are innocent. Judgment is an expression of the separated mind. Throughout the Course, Jesus does not ask us to stop judging; he asks us to be vigilant and to watch ourselves judging and to observe the consequences of our judgments. By definition, judgment leads only to an experience of separation and therefore cannot lead to peace. Since peace is a condition of the return home, judgment needs to be looked at carefully and then released.

Of course, we make judgments all the time; this is simply a necessary feature of life in a body in a world. We judge whether or not it is safe to cross the street, whether we want chicken or salmon for supper, or whether we will get out of bed and go to work in the morning. But these are not the judgments Jesus is referring to. The judgments he wants us to look at are those that reinforce the thought of separation, the judgments that condemn. They are easily recognized by their lack of inclusiveness, reflecting the duality of the split mind, differences, fear, attack, anger, hatred, disgust, aversion, loathing, competition or criticism. He also wants us to look at the judgments that say, "I need this in my life to be happy." If we believe that our peace and happiness depend on something that is in or of the world, we have judged in favour of separation. The only true judgment is the one that says that there is no need to judge, for perfect oneness is all that I seek.

True Purpose

By becoming involved with tangential issues, [the ego] hopes to hide the real question and keep it out of mind. The ego's characteristic busyness with nonessentials is for precisely that purpose. Preoccupations with problems set up to be incapable of solution are favorite ego devices for impeding learning progress. In all these diversionary tactics, however, the one question that is never asked by those who pursue them is, "What for?" This is the question that "you" must learn to ask in connection with everything. What is the purpose? Whatever it is, it will direct your efforts automatically. (T-4.V.6:4–10)

When tragedy strikes or when a challenging or difficult situation arises, it is not uncommon for people to attribute special purpose or meaning to the event. As a way of explaining what has happened, we bravely declare that there must be a good reason for such-and-such or there must be a higher purpose, as though God or some divine force were responsible for our suffering, pain or loss. To think that our problems are happening to us because of some divinely appointed, sacred or holy purpose is naive at best, but clearly insane from the start. From the perspective of the traditional religions and spiritualities of the world, this kind of belief appears to absolve man of any responsibility for some of his greatest tragedies. "Acts of God" imply that our experiences are not our fault. We are the victims. Yet, does anyone ask why God would cause pain and suffering to fall on anyone at all, let alone His Son? What purpose do suffering, sorrow, pain and punishment serve?

> The ego has a purpose, just as the Holy Spirit has. The ego's purpose is fear, because only the fearful can be egotistic. The ego's logic is as impeccable as that of the Holy Spirit, because your mind has the means at its disposal to side with Heaven or earth, as it elects. But again, remember that both are in you. (T-5.V.1:2–5)

From the perspective of *A Course in Miracles* that says God does not know about this world, this line of thinking can have no basis in truth. Nothing that happens in this world to harm, hurt, separate, distinguish, differentiate or divide in any way can be God's plan for His Son. To bring God into the equation does not make sense. God's equation has only one component: oneness. If God does not have a plan or a purpose for this world, who or what does? A universe of such astounding magnitude and complexity must have a truly inspired maker. What is this maker's purpose for this world?

> Projection makes perception. The world you see is what you gave it, nothing more than that. But though it is no more than that, it is not less. Therefore, to you it is important. It is the witness to your state of mind, the outside picture of an inward

condition. As a man thinketh, so does he perceive. (T-21. in.1:1–6)

Essentially, the world as we perceive it—all of it, including its seemingly good parts—is nothing more than a clever device, a mind trick, concocted in the deluded mind of the Son, now asleep and under the sway of the thought system of the ego, as a means of getting rid of his guilt. The whole idea of separation has never left the mind of the Son and remains and always will be but a thought in his mind. Since the world, of which we are one of millions of splintered-off parts, is a projection of the thought of guilt that remains deeply buried in the mind, the world, as we perceive it, is also a good indicator of what is going on in our minds. If we believe in our guilt, we will see a world capable of attack, a world of danger and threat. If we believe in our innocence, we will see a world that calls for love, a world that suffers from the effects of having chosen separation over oneness, but a world incapable of any real danger.

> Every idea has a purpose, and its purpose is always the natural outcome of what it is. Everything that stems from the ego is the natural outcome of its central belief, and the way to undo its results is merely to recognize that their source is not natural, being out of accord with your true nature. (T-11.V.5:1–2)

There is nothing intrinsically divine or holy about what happens in the world; essentially, all of the world's problems stem from our deeply hidden belief in guilt. The rest is nothing more than one huge distraction, whose purpose is to keep us from looking inwards. Fortunately for us, God has nothing to do with this world, nor has He ever had anything to do with it, which means that we are not at the mercy of some omnipotent force beyond our control. However, this means that if what we see is a result of a choice we have made, and continue to make in our mind, then it is our responsibility to find a way to recognize that this is what we are doing, and then to make a different choice.

Two Thought Systems, Two Lenses

> [The Holy Spirit] came into being with the separation as a protection, inspiring the Atonement principle at the same time.... The Holy Spirit is God's Answer to the separation; the means by which the Atonement heals until the whole mind returns to creating.... The Holy Spirit is in you in a very literal sense. His is the Voice that calls you back to where you were before and will be again. (T-5.I.5:2; T-5.II.2:5; 3:7–8)

How do I know whether I am thinking with the ego or with the Holy Spirit? I'm sure there are lots of times when I am thinking with the right mind. I don't spend my days conniving and plotting the death of my enemies, or projecting guilt onto everyone I see. For most of my life, at least until I encountered the Course, I have been a relatively nice, peaceful, kind person. There must be *some* amount of right-minded thinking in me. *A Course in Miracles* helps us distinguish between right- and wrong-minded thinking by pointing out the differences inherent in each thought system and also by directing our attention to the outcome of our choices.

The consequences of that one childish thought that wonders what it might be like to be separate from perfect oneness leads to two possible outcomes, one that is true, the thought system of the Holy Spirit, and the other that is false, the thought system of the ego. One leads to peace, the other reinforces separation. Since the thought of separation leads to two distinct consequences, it shows that what a thought projects is like itself. The thought of separation can only lead to more separation. Thoughts emerging from God's Answer, the Holy Spirit, have never changed and will always reflect the oneness of Heaven. There are essentially only two possible ways, two distinct lenses through which the world can be seen.

The Holy Spirit knows only that which is of God, and since God is Love, he can see nothing other than love. The Holy Spirit says that nothing happened: there was no sin, no need for guilt and certainly no need to fear punishment from God. How could a Son of God possibly be guilty? How could a kind and loving Father even conceive of punishing His Children for something they never did, let alone for something they only imagined? To look with the right-minded lens of the Holy Spirit is to look without judgment, fear, guilt, differences, attack or separation. It is a choice that remains available to us at all times.

HOLY SPIRIT'S VISION

NON-JUDGMENT, SHARED INTERESTS, CALL FOR LOVE

The Holy Spirit, like the ego, is a decision. Together they constitute all the alternatives the mind can accept and obey.... Your decision to see is all that vision requires.... The Holy Spirit's Voice is as loud as your willingness to listen. It cannot be louder without violating your freedom of choice, which the Holy Spirit seeks to restore, never to undermine. (T-5.V.6:6–7; W-pI.20.3:1; T-8.VIII.8:7–8)

When we look through the right-minded lens of the Holy Spirit, or with Jesus, since God is Love, we will see one of two expressions: love or a call for love. Since love is the only true emotion, if a person is not experiencing the Love of God, they must be in pain, since to push away that which is our true inheritance can only lead to lack of peace, pain and loss. When calling for love, we are seeking to recapture that sense of wholeness that was rejected when we, as the one Son, decided to take the thought of separation seriously. To recognize this in our brother is what the Course calls vision. Looking through the lens of the Holy Spirit holds no judgment and leads to a peaceful experience, one that inspires kindness, gentleness and appropriate and helpful action. Right-minded thinking can lead only to thoughts of love, safety, invulnerability, light, abundance, wholeness, shared interests, sameness, all of which are reflections of the perfect oneness of Heaven.

EGO'S PERCEPTION

JUDGMENT, SPECIALNESS, FEAR, SEPARATION, DIFFERENCES

The ego is the part of the mind that believes in division. How could part of God detach itself without believing it is attacking Him?... If you identify with the ego, you must perceive yourself as guilty. Whenever you respond to your ego you will experience guilt, and you will fear punishment. The ego is quite literally a fearful thought. However ridiculous the idea of attacking God may be to the sane mind, never forget that the ego is not sane. It represents a delusional system, and speaks for it. Listening to the ego's voice means that you believe it is possible to attack God, and that a part of Him has been torn away by you. Fear of retaliation from without follows, because the severity of the guilt is so acute that it must be projected. (T-5.V.3:1–2; 5–11)

Jesus makes it clear that if I am not feeling perfect peace, and if I do not feel the same love for everyone, then I must be looking through the only other possible lens: the ego's. If I am not feeling wholly loved, safe and at peace, then most likely I am not looking with the right lens. Why can't looking through the ego's lens lead to an experience of peace? Since thoughts have consequences and these consequences reflect the original thought, and since the original thought made by the separated mind is a thought of separation—essentially an attack thought—whatever comes of this thought must be like itself. The ego's thought system cannot conceive of oneness; it can only conceive of differences, choices, separation, murder, attack, individuality, defensiveness, fear, hatred, judgment, exclusion, competition, opposition, contrast, specialness, conflict, comparison. There is nothing in the fabric of the ego's thought system that can possibly lead to an experience of oneness;

it was conceived as an attack on God and is capable of seeing only differences.

> I have spoken of the ego as if it were a separate thing, acting on its own. This was necessary to persuade you that you cannot dismiss it lightly, and must realize how much of your thinking is ego-directed. (T-4.VI.1:3–4)

Though for teaching purposes, the ego is spoken of as if it appears to have a will and personality of its own, it is simply the result of a choice made in the mind of the Son of God, a way of looking at the world. The ego does not influence us or make us do anything any more than does the man in the moon. It is not a dark spirit, devil or evil force that needs to be educated, controlled, captured or defeated. It simply needs to be looked at for what it is—the result of a choice made in the mind of a child—smiled at and released. The ego's thought system is founded on fear, which is reflected in our basic need to protect and defend ourselves, our families, homes, neighbourhoods and countries against a multitude of potentially dangerous, harmful and life-threatening foes. This defensiveness, based on the fear of punishment for the sin we believe we have committed, extends throughout all levels of worldly life.

From Mindlessness to Mindfulness

> You dream of a separated ego and believe in a world that rests upon it. This is very real to you. You cannot undo it by not changing your mind about it. If you are willing to renounce the role of guardian of your thought system and open it to me, I will correct it very gently and lead you back to God. (T-4.I.4:4–7)

One of the popular phrases of the day is "change your mind, change the world," which is true to a certain extent. If you change your outlook and your attitude, the world will look different and you may be able to effect positive changes in your life. However, working at changing the world is about as effective as watering the oasis; it may get things growing and make a nice oasis, but it will not lead you out of the desert. When Jesus teaches us to change our minds, he does not mean that we should change our minds about anything in the world, change religions or spiritualities, or change for a more positive outlook or attitude about life and abundance. Nor does he ask us to train ourselves to have more peaceful, kind and loving thoughts. This would be an impossible request, since we are not even in touch with the origin of our thoughts, whether kind and loving or mean and hateful. If you wanted to change the direction of the spray of water from a garden sprinkler, you would not do it by directing the water spray with your hands; you would adjust the flow from the control on the sprinkler.

> Whatever you accept into your mind has reality for you. It is your acceptance of it that makes it real. If you enthrone the ego in your mind, your allowing it to enter makes it your reality. This is because the mind is capable of creating reality or making illusions. I said before that you must learn to think with God. To think with Him is to think like Him. This engenders joy, not guilt, because it is natural. Guilt is a sure sign that your thinking is unnatural. Unnatural thinking will always be attended with guilt, because it is the belief in sin. (T-5.V.4:1–9)

Fortunately, Jesus takes us right to the source; he asks us to literally change *minds*. He tells us that we have a right mind and a wrong mind, that it is up to us to realize this, and that it is our responsibility to make a different choice. For that, we must first acknowledge that our thoughts have consequences, that we are responsible for these thoughts and that it is up to us to make a different choice. To reach this place where we know that a different choice can be made, we must be willing to look at what is going on in our mind. Just look. To watch without judgment puts us in our right mind, that place where true power to change the world resides. He asks us to look at the outcomes of our choices, without judgment, and realize that they do not lead to peace. Furthermore, he points out that we have the outcome we desire. Each of our experiences is the result of our decision to choose that experience. If we do not

TWO THOUGHT SYSTEMS

EGO	HOLY SPIRIT
FEAR	LOVE
PERCEPTION	KNOWLEDGE
MULTIPLICITY	ONENESS
JUDGMENT	ACCEPTANCE
COMPLEXITY	SIMPLICITY
NOISINESS	QUIETNESS
SEPARATION	ONENESS
DIVISION	UNITY
AGGRESSIVENESS	GENTLENESS
DIFFERENCES	SAMENESS
SELF-INTERESTS	SHARED INTERESTS
COMPETITION	JOINING
CRITICISM	COMPASSION
ANXIETY	PEACEFULNESS
DEPRESSION	JOY
UNHAPPINESS	CONTENTMENT
SPECIALNESS	HARMONY
SCARCITY, LACK	WHOLENESS
ATTACK	DEFENCELESSNESS
EXCLUSION	INCLUSIVENESS
GREED	DETACHMENT
HATRED	FORGIVENESS
LONELINESS	FAITH

have peace, it is because we did not desire peace. If we have conflict, it is that we desired conflict. If we experience grief, sorrow, loss or pain, it is because, from our ego-thinking mind, in seeking to remain separate, we desired that outcome.

Blindsided by the Ego

> The ego always tries to preserve conflict. It is very ingenious in devising ways that seem to diminish conflict, because it does not want you to find conflict so intolerable that you will insist on giving it up. (T-7.VIII.2:2–3)

The ego is clever. It has only one mode: survive at any cost! There is no fairness or honour in the ego thought system: anything and anyone is fair game so far as its goal of surviving as a special, distinct self is concerned. I realized the extent of its cleverness when, one day, thinking I had responded in a fair way to a minor conflict, it occurred to me that I had been blindsided by the ego. I was becoming a seasoned *Course in Miracles* student; over five years of diligent study. I must be choosing with the right mind.

I don't think anyone would have found fault with my response to my colleague's email, except for Jesus, which he would have done with love and thankfully, without judgment. I was, after all, a student of his Course, and I had already determined that it would be in my best interests to at least try to do what he recommended. But this one slipped by me so quickly that I didn't realize what hit me until I looked back more closely.

I had spent most of the day overhauling the website of an organization for which I volunteered as webmaster. Given the distress in my arms, shoulders and back from years of work at the computer, web design was not my preferred line of work. Nonetheless, it was my plan to set up a blog so that other members could manage the content themselves. Excited to have figured out how to modify the graphics and layout to give it the look and feel that I thought was appropriate, I was in the process of adding finishing touches when I received an email from one of the organization's members. It was a complaint letter, curt and to the point, in which he expressed his extreme frustration with the new site and the precious time wasted in making minor edits to his article—a two-year old article, the only one he had ever contributed to the site. There were no expressions of gratitude for the new site nor thanks for the work. Just a whiny complaint.

I chuckled when I read this email, especially that it arrived within minutes of my having posted the remedy to his very problem. Without a hint of resentment, feeling content with the work I had accomplished that day, I quickly fired off a response that I thought was appropriate. "Hello to you too!" I began. Then I explained that I had just spent six and a half hours working on design and layout and transfer of articles from the old site to the new one so that administrators of the organization could make updates. I told him that I was wearing braces on both wrists and could do without this additional computer work. I'll admit that I was being a bit snarky when I added that I was glad that he liked the new look of the site, and then thanked him. I told him I had just made a correction that would allow him to make his edits. I finished off the whole thing by suggesting that if he didn't like the blog design, he could take over the function of webmaster and use any format that he liked.

Naturally, as a devoted Course student, I re-examined what had occurred, how I had responded and how I felt. Because it was not like me to engage in open conflict, I was intrigued by the fact that I felt satisfied with my response, that I had done the right thing. I even justified my behaviour with the conclusion that perhaps from his ego's perspective he needed to know when he was out of line. However, the more I thought about it, the more the whole situation just did not sit right with me. In the end, this feeling of satisfaction lasted for about a minute and a half. I had not asked Jesus or the Holy Spirit to write this response with me. So, clearly, I had written it with the ego. There was nothing that reflected oneness or shared interests in my email. It was clearly a counterattack in response to a perceived attack.

EGO'S PERCEPTION

DEFENSIVENESS, SEPARATION, ATTACK

No matter how justified I thought I was in putting this person in his place, it still was what it was, an attack response. It was so subtle that the more I thought about it, the angrier I grew with myself, and eventually as the hours passed, I grew angry with Jesus for his damn difficult course. How could anyone learn how to do this properly! It was impossible! Then I recalled what Jesus asks us to do. He asks us to look. And then I reminded myself that if I had been able to look, it meant that I was able to go to that decision-making place in my mind.

This was progress. If I had not known that I had a decision-making place in my mind, I would never get out of it. But now I could stand back and look at it objectively. Yes, I had chosen with the ego's thought system. It had been a very, very clever tactic of the ego. It also occurred to me that I had used the opportunity to project some long-held, but never expressed, feelings toward this person. This was an ego masterpiece! I also recognized the one problem, the mind's decision to remain separate: it was his attack and my counterattack. Either he was right or I was right. Not both. This conflict did not come from a place of love. This was why I felt so uncomfortable for the hours following the incident. I claimed to seek peace, but I had chosen conflict.

In the end, I understood that, now armed with the thought system of the Course, I was able to go back in my mind, understand what had occurred, forgive myself and then return to a more peaceful place. Instead of finding joy in my justified counterattack, I found peace in the knowledge that I could pull myself back far enough, without judgment and with Jesus, and look at the situation differently. This is what he wanted us to do. There was progress; it was slow, but it was there.

HOLY SPIRIT'S VISION

GENTLENESS, DEFENCELESSNESS, UNDERSTANDING

We discussed this event in our *Course in Miracles* study group, as an example of the subtlety of the ego. Someone asked how I might have responded had I addressed the situation with the right mind. Having by then forgiven myself for my mistaken choice, I was able to see clearly how I might have responded had I remembered to look with the Holy Spirit. I could have replied with "Sorry for the inconvenience, I just fixed the problem! Hope you can learn to like the new look." This would have been a kinder response, without a sense of attack-defence, leaving both of us—shared interests—in a far better frame of mind. Next time, I promised myself, I'll try to remember to not function on my own. That seems to get me into trouble.

> We are therefore embarking on an organized, well-struc-tured and carefully planned program aimed at learning how to offer to the Holy Spirit everything you do not want. He knows what to do with it. You do not understand how to use what He knows. Whatever is given Him that is not of God is gone. Yet you must look at it yourself in perfect willingness, for otherwise His knowledge remains useless to you. Surely He will not fail to help you, since help is His only purpose. Do you not have greater reason for fearing the world as you perceive it, than for looking at the cause of fear and letting it go forever? (T-12.II.10:1–7)

Chapter 7

THE BODY: TEMPLE OF THE EGO

The body is the ego's home by its own election. It is the only identification with which the ego feels safe, since the body's vulnerability is its own best argument that you cannot be of God. This is the belief that the ego sponsors eagerly. Yet the ego hates the body, because it cannot accept it as good enough to be its home. (T-4.V.4.1–4)

Fascination with Form

WHO HAS NOT MARVELLED at the wondrous workings of the human body? There is no denying its existence, nor our fervent fascination with it; we see it, feel it and, by our perception of pleasure and pain, judge it as good, bad and altogether impossible to ignore. Whether we love or hate our bodies, whether we have a positive or negative body image, we identify with it as an essential part of who we are. In fact, we believe we are our bodies. Simply recall a time when you were in a crowd, perhaps at a mall, at a show or waiting for a commuter train, and you heard someone call your name. What was your immediate reaction? Unless you were running from the law or your ex, you probably turned toward the voice, raised your hand and waved, attracting the person's attention in the general direction of your body. Here I am!

Most of our life centres on some aspect of the bodily experience. We protect it against the dangers of nature and the world, dress it up, decorate it, pamper it, modify it to our liking, nurture it and tend to its never-ending needs. We get jobs so we can properly feed, shelter and care for our families. We are filled with tears of joy at the sight of a new birth, eager to celebrate the joy of what we call the miracle of life. We devote billions of dollars to study how it works and how to repair and treat it when it breaks down. We produce colourful animation films to teach our children about how all the different parts function together as a harmoniously integrated unit. We just don't show them what a body looks like when it is ill or aging and breaking down.

> The body is the central figure in the dreaming of the world. There is no dream without it, nor does it exist without the dream in which it acts as if it were a person to be seen and be believed. It takes the central place in every dream, which tells the story of how it was made by other bodies, born into the world outside the body, lives a little while and dies, to be united in the dust with other bodies dying like itself. (T-27.VIII.1:1–3)

Through subtle and not-so-subtle body language, we communicate our feelings, intentions and desires to each other, without the need of words. Our choice in clothing, makeup, hairstyle and overall demeanour are said to speak of our inner beliefs about ourselves and our position in the social hierarchies of the world. Before any verbal communication is exchanged, we instinctively respond and react to the bodies of others; there are bodies that appeal to us, attract us and please us, while others disgust and even repulse us. Some bodies stir up feelings of love, protection and nurturing, while there are others we want to destroy, hurt and annihilate. There are bodies we envy, others we desire; body parts we want to show off, others we want to hide in shame. Even in death, our fascination continues, as we dissect our lifeless forms in the name of science, poking and prodding to understand the cause of the loss of this life we hold so precious.

> The Bible says, "The Word (or thought) was made flesh." Strictly speaking this is impossible… Thought cannot be made into flesh except by belief, since thought is not physical…. Any

thought system that confuses God and the body must be insane. (T-8.VII.7:1–2, 4; T-4.V.3:1)

Yet, nobody really questions the origins of this captivating piece of cosmic biology. We simply accept what we are taught, and what we don't know, we attribute to some divine mystery. Why not question its source? We are told that we were created in the image of God. Does anyone not ask of our Maker why He didn't make our bodies perfect, without weaknesses and defects, without its vulnerabilities to millions of dangers? Most of all, why is the body programmed to expire? Whether it dies after forty days or one hundred forty years, it certainly does not reflect the eternal nature of God. This body that interacts with the world outside, this body that answers to calls from within, this body that occupies so much of our time—this form—has nothing of spirit.

If what God creates is like Him, it too must be whole, complete and never in need of anything. But the body is constantly in need, even after the most satisfying meal, we still need to breathe. Even at the cellular level is this state of need reflected, where nourishment from external sources must be ingested, meaning that something must be sacrificed or killed for it to survive. What was consumed is then digested, assimilated, distributed, and what is not needed is expelled as waste. In fact, cellular activity is a remarkable representation of life, not only in a body, but also in the world. Fortunately, Jesus has an answer that makes sense—God did not create the world, much less bodies.

What, No Resistance?

The reader may wonder if I encountered any resistance when it came to writing on the subject of the body from the perspective of the Course, and, truthfully, at least not in the first round of writing, I felt little, if any—only an irresistible urge to devour chocolate chip cookies. It was a number 4 Personal Month of body, health, order, organization and work. I was determined, focused and ready to write, and disciplined enough to limit my cookie consumption to three and a half (there was a broken one in the package that screamed "Eat me, eat me"). Shopping, gardening and baking muffins would come as a reward, but only after the work was complete. Because I identified fully with my self in a body, this was a subject I could address without causing my separated self too much anxiety. Clearly, I wasn't about to morph from matter into spirit and ascend to heaven anytime soon. I had already accepted that I was insane, that I had lost my mind and what kept me in this world was my hidden belief in my inherent sin, guilt and fear. The body was something I could deal with, until I began to really think about what Jesus was telling us in the Course.

It wasn't until the following month, when I returned for another round of edits on this chapter, that the resistance really kicked in, at which time, morning aches and pains really intensified. There was pain in body parts that I didn't know even had pain sensors. I had a free weekend, no clients, no family events, which I eagerly set aside for writing. Two full days! On the Saturday morning, after unfolding my achy body parts out of bed, I did a quick round of grocery shopping, a necessary expenditure of time. Then I worked on the front lawn dethatching the small patches of yellowed grass where I had applied a weed killer. A couple of hours in the garden would do me some good. This precipitated a quick trip to the local garden centre for seed and earth to repair the bare spots on my lawn. Interestingly, crouched over, scraping the grass under the glare of the 34-degree July sun, I felt no pain. Nor was I bothered by the sweat dripping from every pore of my body; heat and hot flashes—my very own sauna.

After lunch, I settled with my laptop in my air-conditioned dining room overlooking the garden. It was a perfect day for writing. Then my back began to ache; I needed more exercise. Off I went for a walk to the corner store for tomatoes, which led to an urge for cedar-planked salmon on the barbeque, despite the severe thunderstorm warning, which wouldn't be a problem since I have a carport. The better part of the afternoon was spent alternating between a couple of minutes at the laptop and preparing the barbecue, soaking the cedar plank, thawing the salmon, making—and nibbling on—a tomato and feta cheese salad with fresh basil from the garden, getting the charcoal going, nibbling some more and, when five o'clock rolled around, sipping a glass of Merlot. By the time the whole affair of preparing and eating was over, I was too stuffed and tired to write, so I settled down to watch a movie and fell asleep.

Some time after ten, as I directed my sleepy body up to bed, I got to thinking about my day and how I had managed to avoid doing what I had originally set out to do. Guilt rose to the surface. So I grabbed the right lens and, without judgment, took a closer look. It did not matter what I did in the world, what mattered was which thought system I chose to interpret what I did. Throughout the day, I had been thinking a lot about my identification with the body, and how this body cannot be who I truly am. I thought about how Jesus is not addressing this person who makes decisions about what to do, when to go shopping and what to make for dinner. He wants us to find that other way of looking, the way that reveals the thought system we have chosen. If I felt guilt, it had nothing to do with whether or not I got my writing done. If I felt guilt it was because I had found an opportunity to project some of my deeply buried guilt outside my mind: an unproductive writing day was just a convenient scapegoat.

Jesus teaches us that the body is an attack on God; this can only lead to feelings of guilt, until one realizes how silly—and arrogant— it is to think that anyone could possibly attack God. Clearly, my daylong musings about the unreality of this body had stirred up some fear, fear that I might get too close to the truth, that we are as God created us, without sin. I could have chosen to spend the day in simple, quiet contemplation, but instead I filled it with bodily activities. I thought about Ramana's complete detachment from the body as he sat for years in silent contemplation. To spend the day in silent contemplation would be too threatening to the survival of my separated ego. As long as I held onto my identification with, and desire for, this separated self, there would be guilt. Guilt means that I believe that I have successfully separated from God. So, yes, understandably, I did encounter resistance. But looked at with the lens of the Holy Spirit, without judgment, at least I knew what I was doing and why. In a way, this was empowering, for it meant that at any time, I could choose differently. It is my choice of thought system that determines how I will feel.

The Body as Symbol of Separation

The body is the ego's idol; the belief in sin made flesh and then projected outward. This produces what seems to be a wall of flesh around the mind, keeping it prisoner in a tiny spot of space and time, beholden unto death, and given but an instant in which to sigh and grieve and die in honor of its master. (T-20.VI.11:1–2)

As we age, most of us have to deal with, at the very least, a few aches and pains, a slower metabolism and less energy. A few days after having written the section in Chapter 1 on how advancing age can motivate us to question the nature of reality, a client who had just turned sixty-two expressed how she felt that more and more attention needed to be paid to the body. By the time we reach fifty or sixty years of age, wise about the world and having tasted most of what life has to offer, many of us want answers that are more substantial than those we were given as children.

One of my daughter's Pilates mentors made the interesting observation that those who tended to be mystical in their youth often have more trouble with their bodies later in life. This is when, after a lifetime spent pursuing worldly goals, we are most likely to turn to the mystical, especially if our learning of the world has left us with lingering unanswered questions. The traditional after-death myths about going home to be with God, where we will joyfully meet up with deceased loved ones and beloved pets, now seem like little more than childish fairy tales.

Our parents are aging, dying or long dead, friends are struggling with life-threatening illnesses and our own body is starting to show the wear of its years. Preoccupied with a variety of symptoms, some more life-threatening or life-altering than others, from arthritis, diabetes, heart conditions and minor aches and pains, to dementia and various forms of cancer, we are certainly not going to be in any condition to consider the possibility that we are spirit. More than ever it seems, the body is front and centre among our priorities and preoccupations, and no matter how kind is our genetics or how much surgery we can afford, the fact remains that, in the end, the body will fail and we will cease to exist in form. So why is it that, at the one time in our life when we are most likely to question the nature of our existence, our bodies start to fail and require much, if not all, of our attention, so that gerontological issues leave little or no time for ontological exploration?

Another challenging aspect of the teachings of A Course in Miracles is that it states that God made neither the world nor the body. The body, the Course tells us, is the domain of the ego, an "engine of destruction." That being true, it then cannot be of God, for a choice for the ego is a choice against God. Essentially, the body is an attack on God. Its purpose is to keep us separate from others. Where there is separation, God cannot be. Once identified with a body, we no longer have any memory of our true Self as Spirit. Since the body is a conception of the ego, made to establish and maintain our belief in separation, it makes sense that it would have a built-in safety mechanism designed to ensure against our ever questioning of its origins or, heaven forbid, true purpose. An aging and failing body does an excellent job of keeping us from the truth.

> The ego uses the body to conspire against your mind, and because the ego realizes that its "enemy" can end them both merely by recognizing they are not part of you, they join in the attack together. This is perhaps the strangest perception of all, if you consider what it really involves. The ego, which is not real, attempts to persuade the mind, which is real, that the mind is the ego's learning device; and further, that the body is more real than the mind is. No one in his right mind could possibly believe this, and no one in his right mind does believe it. (T-6.IV.5:1–4)

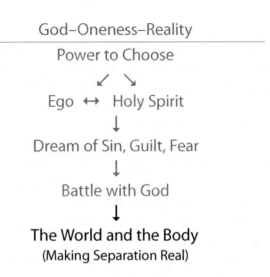

God–Oneness–Reality

Power to Choose

Ego ↔ Holy Spirit

Dream of Sin, Guilt, Fear

Battle with God

The World and the Body
(Making Separation Real)

That the body is an expression of the thought of separation is evident when we consider how it is conceived. One sperm, after beating out hundreds of other sperm in a race to the egg, successfully penetrates and fertilizes the egg, clearly an attempt at joining that which is separate. Joined for a moment as one, they do a little dance and, before you know it, they begin splitting into hundreds of cells. The first marriage has spawned the first divorce long before the child is even born. The cells continue to divide and organize themselves according to special functions, further establishing separation and introducing hierarchies, since some body organs and functions will be more important than others. The birthing process itself, usually a painful ordeal for the mother, is a symbol of the original thought that says that it is possible to separate from perfect oneness. The fetus—once safe in the womb where all of its needs were met—has now been thrust out into a world in which it must struggle for its very survival. Wholeness no longer exists; separation appears to be real.

From the moment we are born, we are in a state of lack; we need air, water and food, without which we will die. The separated self then proceeds to spend the rest of its life ensuring its survival and attempting to find some semblance of wholeness. When old enough, we set out to attract the perfect mate, the one who will heal our deep feelings of abandonment, rejection and separation. The joy we experience at the sight of a childbirth can belong only to a mind that believes in the thought system of the ego. It says that separation is possible. Here is irrefutable proof. It does not matter that spirit has once again been abandoned and replaced by a body; what matters is that separation has been made real. The war against God has once again been won.

> The ability to perceive made the body possible, because you must perceive *something* and *with* something. (T-3.IV.6:1)

The body is a multi-faceted device and serves many purposes, many of which we are entirely unaware. It is equipped with senses and a brain, a sophisticated system for gathering and processing information that functions at all times, even as we sleep. Besides acting as a vehicle for our experience as separated selves, the body provides pleasure, further luring us into its grip. While for the most part we would claim to want to maximize pleasure and minimize pain, there are times when pain has its benefits. In fact, pain, whether physical or emotional, serves some very special and unique functions in the ego's thought system. If my sensory apparatus reports pain signals back to my brain, this reinforces that I am in a body and therefore separate. If I suffer in any way, this means that someone or something outside of me is inflicting pain on me, proving, yet again, that there is a "me." Suffering at the hands of any kind of external source, be it a person, thing or even a micro-organism that has attacked my immune system, also puts me in the position of victim. I can justly say that my suffering is not my fault. This reinforces my strong need to believe in my innocence, which, from the perspective of the ego, is achieved by making someone or something else guilty.

Another benefit of suffering, be it any form of illness or pain, is that it provides me with some of the punishment I feel I deserve for my innate sinfulness. This pain or illness will buy me some time; God will not require punishment for my sin since I am already suffering, besides which, I am suffering at the hands of another. In the end, suffering, illness and pain are very important components of life in a body as seen through the lens of the ego.

The Paradox of the Healer

> The acceptance of sickness as a decision of the mind, for a purpose for which it would use the body, is the basis of healing. And this is so for healing in all forms. A patient decides that this is so, and he recovers. If he decides against recovery, he will not be healed. Who is the physician? Only the mind of the patient himself. The outcome is what he decides that it is. Special agents seem to be ministering to him, yet they but give form to his own choice. He chooses them in order to bring tangible form to his desires. And it is this they do, and nothing else. They are not actually needed at all. The patient could merely rise up without their aid and say, "I have no use for this." There is no form of sickness that would not be cured at once. (M-5.II.2:1–13)

When I was young, I was in awe of healers like Jesus, Brother Andre and Padre Pio; in fact, I believed that healing was the greatest of gifts. Over the years, I studied many of the alternative healing arts, at first for my own healing and later to heal my daughters of the common ailments encountered in childhood. It never occurred to me that my heroes had not pursued special training in healing; they simply healed from the heart, love being the most powerful healer. Looked at from the perspective of *A Course in Miracles*, the subject of the body, illness and healing can be somewhat confounding for practitioners of the healing arts, in particular, the alternative healing arts.

I have seen many students quit very early in their work with the Course, dismayed on seeing their life's work apparently in conflict with the unusual teachings of the Course. Their reaction is not entirely unreasonable when you consider statements such as Lesson 136 which says that sickness is a defence against the truth or that sickness is a decision of the mind and serves a very specific purpose.

What is a well-intentioned reiki master or reflexologist to do with such a teaching?

Healers are motivated by a sincere desire to bring wellness to a patient, and hopefully to effect healing and remove pain, discomfort and illness. They believe their learning, energy, power and skill will make the healing happen. Alternative health practitioners in particular, also believe there is a direct link between the health of the body and states of mind and emotions. They might say, for example, that fear is what has caused a problem with the kidneys or grief is what caused a problem with the heart. This kind of thinking, though it makes sense for a figure in a dream, does not go to the real cause of the illness, which, the Course says, is a decision made in the mind to push away the truth. The real fear belongs to the ego, the fear that we might look inside and discover the truth of our innocence, that we are spirit and not bodies, and that there is no need to suffer punishment for a sin we have not committed. Illness keeps us in the body; the body shields us from the Love of God.

Additionally, the Course tells us that healing does not come from the healer; rather, it comes from the mind of the patient who decided to be ill in the first place. Sickness is a decision and serves a purpose. Anything that brings attention to the body serves the ego's purpose, which is to ensure that we continue to identify with our separated selves as bodies, and not as spirit. For some patients, illness becomes a part of who they are, especially those suffering from long-term or chronic illnesses. As long as the illness serves the ego's purpose, no amount of energy or healing skill will heal the patient. To attempt to remove the illness before the patient is ready is basically a waste of time and resources. All healing remains in the mind of the patient, where the decision to be ill was made. When the patient is ready to heal, they will consult a practitioner— whether allopathic or alternative, it does not matter at all which form they choose—and they will obtain the healing they seek. This is why no healing approach works all the time with all patients. This is also why some patients appear to miraculously recover from life-threatening conditions, while others succumb.

This new perspective on healing and sickness requires a significant readjustment in the outlook of the healer, one that is almost
impossible to achieve without a thorough understanding and
acceptance of the metaphysics of the Course. The healer simply
facilitates the patient's desired outcome. "Your wish is my com-
mand." When illness no longer serves the ego's purpose, illness
goes away. Medicine or therapy is needed only because the idea of
spontaneous healing would be too frightening to the patient. The
best approach for the health practitioner is simply to practise their
profession simply for the love of it. Patients will come when they
are ready to be healed. That way, the burden of healing is not on
the healer.

Since the function of the student of *A Course in Miracles* is
simply to be a representative for the other way of seeing, the practice of healing, in whichever form it takes, becomes an opportunity
for the healer to practise looking through the non-judgmental lens
of the Holy Spirit. While watching for thoughts of separation, pity,
judgment or any thoughts that bear even a hint of differences, it is,
in effect, the mind of the healer that is being healed. Since minds are
joined, the patient will take whatever learning is desired at that particular time. It is not the function of the healer to determine what
the patient needs to learn, nor how they will heal; that is between
the patient and the Holy Spirit. It is the healer's function to look
with the eyes of vision, to look beyond the body and to see that we
are all split off parts of the same decision for separation, all longing
to know that there is a way to return to our true home, with God.

Healing must occur in exact proportion to which the val-
uelessness of sickness is recognized. One need but say, "There
is no gain at all to me in this" and he is healed. But to say this,
one first must recognize certain facts. First, it is obvious that
decisions are of the mind, not of the body. If sickness is but a
faulty problem-solving approach, it is a decision. And if it is
a decision, it is the mind and not the body that makes it. The
resistance to recognizing this is enormous, because the exis-

tence of the world as you perceive it depends on the body being the decision maker. (M-5.II.1:1–7)

A Decision for Healing

In the fall of 2009, I began to experience severe pain in my upper back, shoulders and arms, especially my right arm, to the point where I could barely raise it to shoulder level. It had been six months since my mom had moved in and, above my usual work at the computer, we had been busy with all sorts of renovations around the house. At this point, any halfway competent health practitioner would want to know a bit about my relationship with my mom and, from the usual perspective of the world, this would appear to be a sound approach for evaluating my health issues. Suffice it to say that being of completely different temperaments and sharing very few common views, my mom and I were not the closest of mother–daughter duos. Since she had moved in, we had already experienced a couple of unpleasant encounters, following which I decided that I would, at all costs, avoid further confrontation.

The cost of keeping my grievances to myself, it appeared, was pain in my body. A lot of mileage could be derived from the symbolism of this condition, for example, paralyzing pain in the arms representing powerlessness, etc. But I did not want to go down that road. I wanted to go to the source of the pain and experience true healing. Until my goal was achieved, I dealt with the situation as best as I could, avoiding open confrontation, focusing on my work, going for long walks and listening to many hours of Ken Wapnick workshops. As for the rest, I tried to be as kind and patient as I could be. For the most part, life with my mom was, though not filled with warmth and love, at least livable.

It was another of those mornings when I woke up feeling the pains of excessive stress and tension accumulated in my back and shoulders. I had attended a Body Rolling workshop given by my daughter the previous Saturday, which required driving into town, further aggravating my right arm from handling the gear shift, and then had spent the Sunday doing a small fall cleanup in the garden. I knew that my time in the garden would be paid for with pain during the night, but it didn't matter; time in the garden is always a peaceful interlude. Then I realized that it was Monday morning. How would I get through yoga class with all that pain in my shoulders and back? Before leaving, with my yoga mat packed and ready to go, I decided to read a Course lesson. It was with a profound feeling of peace and especially hope that I read Lesson 75. More and more, I was starting to believe that through the practice of the Course, it would actually be possible to reach the goal of awakening from the dream.

The light has come. I have forgiven the world. (W.pI.75)

I mulled over these words, savouring the hope they carried when I experienced a momentary flash, an understanding that went far beyond anything I could express in words, a sense of promise—a promise made, a promise kept. It was one of those moments in which I envied the great poets for their ability to put into words experiences that do not belong in words. So it was, filled with the hope of my lesson of the day that I walked to yoga class that morning. Perhaps I would come to understand what it was that I needed to do to heal my body of its pains, or perhaps I just needed to observe the pain and be with it. When I arrived at yoga class, my teacher, Bhaskar, pointed out that it was Divali, the Hindu Festival of Lights. The light has come, I thought to myself.

Although I did not expect to do much of the class that morning, I was pleasantly surprised to find that I was able to keep up with most of the hour-and-a-half Hatha yoga session. As was my custom in yoga class, I surrendered myself completely to the poses. I was by far not a very accomplished yoga practitioner; in fact, I am about as flexible as a wooden chair, but I understood that, at least for me, yoga was about surrender, not gymnastics. By practising the art of surrender, I was preparing the way for my return home. That's all that mattered. As I let myself flow through the postures, I felt my attention drifting away, beyond the present time, and again, as frequently happened during yoga, images of lives past came into my awareness, lives spent in yogic and other contemplative practices.

Then it began to occur to me that the pains felt in my back might be related to experiences from lives lived long ago. Surrendering further into my relaxation, I waited quietly for the next image to arise. In it I saw myself as a spiritual seeker who was very desirous of experiencing enlightenment. In that life, I had pushed very hard, applying myself with almost brutal discipline, unaware that my perseverance was motivated by my unconscious belief in my guilt, a guilt that was deserving of severe punishment. It was this belief that drove me to the extreme practices that ultimately led to severe back pain, drawing my attention into the body, directing it away from my goal.

Then I thought of the Course, and how clear it is from this wonderful teaching that anything that is of God can only be whole and innocent. It is in my innocence that I am as God created me. If there is pain, there is belief in guilt, which is as the ego would like me to believe. But since I cannot be other than as God created me, even as I continue to choose to believe in my guilt, it does not change who I really am, a Child of God. The only thing I needed to do was to forgive myself for holding on to the belief that I could be anything other than innocent. In that moment, I experienced a profound and tearful release. For truly, how could God have the slightest punishing intent toward His Child who is created of His wholeness and perfection? How could God wish anything but love for His Creation?

Despite my yoga practice, the pain in my right arm and shoulder continued, but while I might have been discouraged with my lack of progress, I understood that the discomfort I experienced was a reflection of the inner conflict between my desire to choose with the right mind and my fear of losing my identification with this seemingly separated self in a body. Though I understood the problem on a deeper, metaphysical level, in the world of form, I needed to deal with it in a normal manner, so I made an appointment with my osteopath. Isabel is a seasoned health practitioner, and also very intuitive. I had to laugh when, as she worked my arm and shoulder, she remarked that my heart was closed off, a rather accurate observation given my current living arrangement. Yes, my heart was closed off to love in my relationship with my mother, and in all relationships, for that matter. I knew that. When these treatments failed to relieve the pain, I moved on to a shiatsu therapist, conveniently recommended by a client who had just happened to drop by at the time when I was looking for another solution.

I went for several sessions of wonderful shiatsu, with some benefit, but the pain in the right arm just would not budge. Growing discouraged with our lack of progress, Yutaka, a Buddhist, remarked that I was holding on to the pain. Feeling bad, and not wanting him to second guess his tremendous skill, I told him, in his language, that I was very much aware of my fear of letting go and embracing the Pure Land, what I understood to be the Buddhist equivalent of the Real World of *A Course in Miracles*. Over a period of several weeks, no doubt prompted by the combination of yoga practice, shiatsu and meditation, I experienced several, what can only be described as, semi-veiled recollections. These images usually came during the quiet moments following yoga practice, as I sat peacefully on my Zen bench, and they all centred on variations of the same theme that seemed to have been started at yoga class on the day of the Festival of Lights. I caught glimpses of myself as a monk in different times and locations, usually hundreds of years ago, either in China, Tibet or India. I saw flashes of having come down from a mountain retreat only to discover that my family had been slaughtered. It was guilt that eventually consumed me. In other images, I saw myself lying in the dirt, a beggar, being stomped on by vicious attackers until my back was broken and bent.

These veiled flashbacks became the backdrop onto which were projected my usual daily activities, my work, consultations and life with mom. The lifelong quest of my present life made sense, and the physical pain certainly seemed to have foundations in the past. Meanwhile, I found it necessary to reduce my driving time to as few outings as possible, for each time I took the car out, the pain in my arm kept me awake at night. This meant that I could not take my mom shopping, something she enjoyed very much. With no progress being made with the healing of my arm, and no benefits coming from the memory images, I decided that I'd had enough of the whole business. The pain was becoming an inconvenience, for myself, but especially for my mom. I decided that there must be a better way of resisting the message of the Course.

First of all, the trips down oriental memory lane served no good purpose; in fact, they just reinforced my bodily identification and, on top of that, made me a victim of circumstances that appeared to be beyond my control. This would have to stop. No more visions; no more past life tours. If there was pain, it was because I was pushing away the Love of God, not because of something that may or may not have happened three hundred years ago on a dusty Tibetan roadside. That was enough, and besides that, I told Jesus one night, this whole business of not being able to drive my mom around was not very helpful. My resistance would have to find a means of expression that did not inconvenience her.

I believe it was the following morning, or perhaps the next one, that I awoke with the very clear idea that I should give Robert, the *ramancheur*,[1] a call. As he was not home, I left a message, but immediately after making the call, I decided that I would not be able to make the long drive to Sorel—the pain was in my gear-shifting arm. When he returned my call the following day, he reminded me of what might happen if I did not address the problem soon. Picturing my permanently frozen shoulder, I had to agree. My next concern was the long drive. I thought of the pain, but then I thought of the eventual permanent damage and decided to take my chances with the long drive.

It was a lovely autumn day, and my mom came along for the drive. It was a Saturday morning, and the drive went very smoothly. No traffic, no stops, very few shifts of the gears. In fact, I didn't feel

---

1. As told in Chapter 13 of *Making Peace with God*, a *ramancheur* is a French-Canadian term for a folk healer.

any shoulder pain during the entire drive. This time the session with Robert was much less painful than it had been in 2007. It was painful, but I didn't scream and I didn't go into shock. According to Robert, my arm had slipped out of its shoulder socket—one strong, swift manipulation and it was reset. As simple as that. During our visit, Robert also reset a painful joint in my mom's foot. All in all, it had been a very fruitful visit.

Though I was very much appreciative of the release from intense pain, I knew that this was only a Band-Aid over a much deeper problem. There were still the hot flashes and what I had come to call "carpal tunnel upper body," the various aches and pains I suffered from too many hours sitting at the computer. But I could live with those. They were simply a reminder of my identification with my self as a body. Best of all, I was able to drive again, and my mom really enjoyed our outings. The holidays were just around the corner; being able to drive would be a definite asset.

A Course in Mind Training, Not Body Control

A Course in Miracles is a course in mind training and has absolutely nothing to do with the body. While some spiritual practices involve the control and discipline of the body, the Course does not require any such focus of its students. What Jesus asks of his students is that we be vigilant for our motivations. What is it for? What is the purpose? Does this serve the ego's agenda or the Holy Spirit's? The condition of the body has nothing to do with the state of spirit. Some of the most highly advanced spiritual students and teachers have suffered great physical trauma and illness. To measure spiritual progress against physical health is silly. A healthy body is not a requirement for returning Home. In fact, most spiritualities teach that detachment from all that concerns the body will facilitate our release from the illusion of the world.

Near the end of his life, Ramana's body became infected by a tumour that developed into a sarcoma. Sensing that he would soon die, his devotees expressed their grief, pleading with him to take medicine to make his body whole. Ramana tried to relieve their sadness by pointing out the meaninglessness of the body.

"You attach too much importance to the body … They say that I am dying but I am not going away. Where could I go? I am here."[2]

The Course leads us to the understanding that we have chosen to identify with a bodily form in order to keep the Love of God away. It teaches that we are spirit; that bodies are not real. When we understand that we are spirit, what does it matter what happens to the body? We are not the body. The body has no life; it simply serves the ego's purpose of maintaining separation. True life is spirit.

God Has No Teeth!

It was late April, and I had a 9:30 consultation to prepare, but I had promised myself to make time for a yoga practice before I settled down at the computer. I let the cat out, turned on the space heater in the yoga room downstairs, got dressed, checked my email, and then was ready for yoga. While doing all that, it occurred to me that I should read my lesson for the day so that I could ponder over it during my practice. I headed downstairs and began to do a few warm-up stretches only to realize I had forgotten to read my lesson. I went upstairs, got the coffee ready to go, cleared a couple of dishes out of the sink, returned downstairs, resumed my warm-ups and realized that I had forgotten to read my lesson. I returned upstairs, checked to see if the cat wanted to come back in, returned downstairs for my yoga practice, resumed my warm-ups and realized I had yet again forgotten to read my lesson. I laughed as I went back upstairs recognizing my resistance to continuing my work with the Course. It was a beautiful lesson and clearly my ego-identified self wanted no part of it.

---

2. Arthur Osborne, *Ramana Maharshi and the Path of Self-Knowledge*, page 185.

God, being Love, is also happiness.

To fear Him is to be afraid of joy.
God, being Love, is also happiness.
And it is happiness I seek today.
I cannot fail, because I seek the truth. (W-pI.103.2:5, 3:5–7)

That day, I had decided to practice without a DVD. While listening to the enchanting strains of my favourite yoga music, I returned to my warm-up and slowly moved into sun salutations. My yoga practice was far from being a pretty sight; it would no doubt be the horror of any half-serious yoga teacher. But for me, it was a precious quiet time when I felt close to God. It was a few minutes when the insanity of the world seemed to not cave in on me. Yoga was not about the poses; yoga was about union. It was also a time when I could stretch my body, work out the aches and pains that had been steadily building up over the years. There was no need for me to suffer stiffness and tension and pain, and at that moment, I joined with all the yoga masters from long ago. I felt the power of yoga as I moved awkwardly through my poses, moving with my breath in and out, working out the tensions and stiffness in my body. As long as I believed myself to be in a body, I needed to take care of it so that I could continue with my true work of forgiveness, not because God wills it or because He gave me this body.

I thought of my lesson of the day, and understood that the happiness God wills for us is not the happiness of doing a perfect backbend. The happiness He wills for us is achieved only once we have removed enough of the fear so that we can accept our true place in heaven. The happiness God wills for us is forever. The happiness God wills for us cannot come from anything in and of this world. Then I caught a momentary glimpse of that true life in heaven, my true life free of the burdens and chains of life in the world in a body. I felt the lifting of huge weights in me, around me, on me, and I wept. It was not about the Course, it was not about the body, it was not about yoga. What and whom I considered myself to be in this world in this body disappeared for a moment, and I wept some more. I held on to this experience for as long as I could for the remainder of my practice, knowing full well that I would lose it once I returned to my daily activities. Yet, I knew that I was one step closer; I knew that what I was learning and practising in the Course was working. I wept some more. They were tears of release, tears of joy, tears of longing for what I believed I had lost, but for what I knew was just an arm's length away—God's arm, reaching out to me, patiently waiting for the moment when I will have released all fear.

Of course, the wonderful state I experienced did not last all day; in fact, it barely lasted a few minutes as I left the yoga room and ate my breakfast so that I could prepare for my consultation. Early in the afternoon I was sitting in the dentist's chair recalling my lesson of the day and remembering how God wants me to be happy. Something that is kind of difficult to do with mirrors and hoses and drills buzzing around your mouth. I was tense; I dislike going to the dentist almost as much as I dislike going to the gynecologist. And then I thought, where there is pain there is no God. Where there is God there is no pain. The only logical conclusion was that God has no teeth. I thought about this as the dental hygienist scraped the tea stains off my teeth, and I almost burst out laughing, which would not have been a good idea, since somebody—not me—would have been attacked by a hose and a drill and whatever other devices were in my mouth. So I laughed silently. I knew that I was fully identified with the body. On the way home, I returned to that state of grace, thinking of the day when I would take his hand and go home. It was a good feeling. There was true hope.

When your body and your ego and your dreams are gone, you will know that you will last forever. Perhaps you think this is accomplished through death, but nothing is accomplished through death, because death is nothing. Everything is accomplished through life, and life is of the mind and in the mind. The body neither lives nor dies, because it cannot contain you who are life. (T-6.V.A.1:1–4)

Chapter 8

THE MIRACLE OF FORGIVENESS

When you meet anyone, remember it is a holy encounter. As you see him you will see yourself. As you treat him you will treat yourself. As you think of him you will think of yourself. Never forget this, for in him you will find yourself or lose yourself. Whenever two Sons of God meet, they are given another chance at salvation. Do not leave anyone without giving salvation to him and receiving it yourself. For I am always there with you, in remembrance of *you*. (T-8.III.4:1–8)

Shades of Unforgiveness

THOUGH INTELLECTUALLY CHALLENGING AND without a doubt a stimulating topic of conversation among aficionados, without practical application, the study of *A Course in Miracles* remains just that, a topic of conversation. The process of learning the Course is a bit like learning to read and write, where at first we learned the letters of the alphabet, which were then joined to make words, then sentences, which grew into paragraphs. Over the years, we applied this skill to communicate and interact with the world around us, opening up endless possibilities for further learning and interaction. Similarly with the Course, the student begins by becoming familiar with its language and metaphysics. Since the goal of the Course is to help us awaken from the dream, naturally, the next step would be to apply it in our lives. However, given that the Course is designed to undo everything we have learned to be true about ourselves and the world, contrary to learning to read and write, its students are very likely to encounter profound resistance when it comes to its application. It is much easier, and far less disturbing, to just talk about it, quote nice passages here and there, and pretend to be on a lovely spiritual journey. However, without direct application, no one is leaving the desert anytime soon.

> In looking at the special relationship, it is necessary first to realize that it involves a great amount of pain. Anxiety, despair, guilt and attack all enter into it, broken into by periods in which they seem to be gone. All these must be understood for what they are. Whatever form they take, they are always an attack on the self to make the other guilty. (T-16.V.1:1–4)

Forgiveness and special relationships are like the paragraphs of *A Course in Miracles*, subjects that at first I found to be particularly difficult to grasp. As far as I was concerned, I had altogether dealt with the matter by making certain that I had as few special relationships as possible, which meant there was really not anything or anyone to forgive. My share of failed partnerships had taught me that it was much simpler to do without. Having long outgrown my codependency issues, there was no urgent desire to have a partner. Special love relationships were just too complicated; I wanted a simple, peaceful life, which is more or less what I had.

Far from being a recluse, I met hundreds of people each year through consultations, workshops and business networking events, interactions that I very much enjoyed. In fact, I cared very much for my clients, feeling for their difficulties and challenges and rooting for their success, happiness and achievements. As a result, over the years I developed many great friendships. Then there were my daughters, my favourite special relationships, whom I love very much and whose company I thoroughly enjoy. Very proud of them, I also feel very blessed to have them in my life. So, all and all, I believed that there were no real special relationship issues in my life. Except for the one relationship that remained in the shadows of unforgiveness, the healing of which would become an integral part of my learning process with *A Course in Miracles*.

This tiny spot of sin that stands between you and your brother still is holding back the happy opening of Heaven's gate. How little is the hindrance that withholds the wealth of Heaven from you. And how great will be the joy in Heaven when you join the mighty chorus to the Love of God! (T-26. IV.6:1–3)

By early 2010, I had managed to recover some of my distinguished disposition, the drunken sailor having pretty much pulled up anchor and the bitch ninny having vented herself into little more than a silly memory. Although I was feeling a deeper sense of peace, a dull weariness was making its way into my awareness, and so I was not yet a happy learner. I recalled the line in the Manual that says that time winds on wearily and that the world is tired, but with a lifelong journey behind me, I felt as though *I* wound on wearily and was spiritually tired.

My mom and I had settled into a comfortable routine. I worked a lot; she did crossword puzzles and read. She seemed sad. It was difficult to find a subject of conversation that did not reflect our diametrically opposed points of view and stir up disagreement, so, for the most part, I avoided any potentially inflammatory topics. Sometimes I simply agreed, even if I totally disagreed. We cooked and experimented with new recipes, something we both very much enjoyed, and on the weekends, we went shopping and watched television shows I had recorded during the week. Sometimes I was able to make her laugh with my silly comments about my mangy cat Maggie, the neurotic neighbour across the street, the wacky weather or some other completely innocuous subject. She would laugh when I did my daily arm and shoulder shaking and rolling routine, a habit I had developed to help with the perennial pain and tension in my body from too many hours at the computer. Her musical laughter was the most delightful sound in the house, and I thanked Jesus every time I was blessed with its joyful refrain. Yet for all its apparent civility, this remained a strained relationship.

Every brother you meet becomes a witness for Christ or for the ego, depending on what you perceive in him. Everyone convinces you of what you want to perceive, and of the reality of the kingdom you have chosen for your vigilance. Everything you perceive is a witness to the thought system you want to be true. Every brother has the power to release you, if you choose to be free. You cannot accept false witness of him unless you have evoked false witnesses against him. If he speaks not of Christ to you, you spoke not of Christ to him. You hear but your own voice, and if Christ speaks through you, you will hear Him. (T-11.V.18:1–7)

No one can enter heaven by himself, Jesus tells us in the Course, words that danced devilishly in the back of my mind, which, admittedly, I found distressing. Fiercely independent and self-reliant, I think I believed that I could race right out of the desert and knock on heaven's door all by myself, leaving behind everyone and all the hassles and complications of personal relationships. My spiritual journey was mine alone; it was private and it did not need to include anyone else. Besides, other than our little Thursday evening study group, there was no one in my immediate circle of family and friends who was interested in *A Course in Miracles*, no one with whom to share the journey. Evidently, I had made my journey with the Course special and still identified with the ego's thought system. I was using it to protect and maintain my separateness, an attitude that was not going to get me very far out of the desert, an attitude that would have to be looked into. Since special relationships are really where the application of the Course happens, I encountered very little resistance to working on this section. In fact, I think I was growing tired of my resistance. It was time to move forward with my healing process.

What really pushed me on my journey was the horrifying discovery of the deep feelings of resentment and hatred I harboured toward my mom. It was a dark part of my mind that I wished I could instantly erase, but it remained, a festering open sore that just would not heal. This was not a holy relationship; it was not even a happy relationship. Unsuccessful in my efforts to feel love for my mother, I began to think that I would never get beyond our separateness, and so would never get very far with the Course. I concluded that I was not advanced enough in my learning and understanding of the Course to heal this relationship.

> Be not afraid to look upon the special hate relationship, for freedom lies in looking at it. It would be impossible not to know the meaning of love, except for this. (T-16.IV.1:1–2)

Disheartened, one night I told Jesus how I felt and that I thought that this situation really needed to change. This was not a healthy environment for my mom; clearly, she was not happy. I needed help in learning how to relinquish the ancient grievances that held my heart hostage. I wanted my brother to speak of Christ to me. A week or so afterwards, while thinking that I might not be up to this challenge, all of a sudden, the thought occurred that perhaps I was more afraid that I could actually *be* successful with the Course's teaching. Instantly, I felt a gush of hope. Yes, I can do this, I thought, and with renewed courage, I redoubled my efforts at trying to better understand and apply the miracle teachings of the Course.

> One source of perceived discouragement from which you may suffer is your belief that this takes time, and that the results of the Holy Spirit's teachings are far in the future. This is not so. For the Holy Spirit uses time in His Own way, and is not bound by it. (T-15.I.2:1–3)

The Special Relationship

The subject of special relationships is perhaps by far the most challenging aspect of the Course's teachings, one that most students would simply prefer to skip over. The special relationship is a clever device of the ego. What is of God is one, whole, complete and the same; what is of the ego is separate and distinct. Nothing that is of God can be special, for specialness implies differences. What is special must be of the ego. Our first special relationship begins when we, as the one Son, chose the ego's crazy idea of separation over the Holy Spirit's Answer of oneness. In order to maintain separation, allegiance to the ego's thought system is required. By now, we know the story quite well. Since the Son, believing in his inherent sinfulness, fears punishment from God, his next very special relationship is with God, whom he fears and even hates for the life He can take from him. The Son has forgotten that his only true relationship is with God, a relationship of perfect love. As a separated Son, a relationship with God cannot be a loving one.

> The search for the special relationship is the sign that you equate yourself with the ego and not with God. For the special relationship has value only to the ego. To the ego, unless a relationship has special value it has no meaning, for it perceives all love as special. Yet this cannot be natural, for it is unlike the relationship of God and His Son, and all relationships that are unlike this one must be unnatural. For God created love as He would have it be, and gave it as it is. Love has no meaning except as its Creator defined it by His Will. It is impossible to define it otherwise and understand it. (T-16.VI.1:1–7)

To ensure that the Son remains mindless, the ego makes up a world in which he can hide from God, and just to make extra certain that the Son does not look inward and uncover the truth of his sinlessness, the ego gives him a body that will keep him very, very occupied. Our next special relationship is with our body. No one can deny this special relationship. I need air to breathe, I need food and water, I am a diabetic, I am cold, I need a sweater, my body requires certain foods, I am allergic to peanuts, I need my coffee, I need my eight hours of sleep, I am having a hot flash. Every body has special requirements. This special relationship is so total and all-consuming that we actually believe that we are our body.

Our next special relationship is with our parents, or those persons who first took care of us after we were born. In order to respect our commitment to our separated selves in bodies, we learned to do whatever it took in order to have our basic survival needs met. As infants, we yelled, screamed, cried, smiled, manipulated, complied—whatever it took to be fed and nurtured. When our needs were met, at least until the next need surfaced, we felt loved; when they were not met, we felt abandoned and rejected. These early interactions established many of the patterns that have remained with us for most of our lives. Having no recollection of our true home with our Father in heaven, we learned to interact and compete effectively in a world of differences and separation.

Then we fall in love, we see something in another person that is like us; he is just like me, we both like the same music, she likes to sail, he loves children, we had similar childhoods, we are soulmates. The special other often has the added appeal of offering something that we lack, such as a skill, a quality or certain life experiences, and we now feel complete, whole. This special person will give me something my parents withheld from me. As the relationship develops and we get to know the person better, the ego begins to work its magic, looking for opportunities for projecting pent-up guilt. In time, what was once cute and endearing begins to grate on our nerves while less appealing facets of the personality rise to the surface.

In order to keep the illusion of love going, we keep the negative traits hidden for as long as possible, but because this is a love based on specialness, eventually they will become impossible to ignore. Conflict creeps in where love once made the world go round. Now we have the makings of the perfect special relationship, for we have someone we can blame for our unhappiness. The couple settles into a pattern of victim–victimizer, the roles often switching from one to the other. The special relationship has become a full-fledged ego device, perfect for projecting guilt, the ideal set-up for keeping the focus outside the mind, away from the true problem, which is the mind's decision for guilt.

We say that relationships are about compromise, the balance between give and take. In a special love relationship, we give something of ourselves to another, yet we do not stop to ponder what it is that we give. If our existence as a separated self was purchased at the cost of the Love of God, this self, of which we give, cannot really be of great value. In fact, as we believe this self to be sinful and guilty, it can only be deserving of loathing, not love. If this is our deepest belief about ourselves, we must be giving away what we do not want. What manner of gift is this?

Jesus tells us that peace is a condition for entering the Kingdom of Heaven; therefore, peace must be a threat to the ego's thought system. In a world that was not made by God, peace must be replaced by its opposite, drowned out by noise, conflict, hatred, threat, danger. When relationships end, they rarely do so peacefully, divorce being a prime example of the ego's thought system in its full divisive glory. Parties are required to choose sides and break ties with long-held relationships; children must divide their loyalties between their parents. From the perspective of the Course, it becomes clear that the true source of the anger, resentment and especially the guilt that emerges during a divorce arises from the hidden guilt over the original thought of separation, our divorce from God. This is why divorce is such a guilt-filled, conflict-ridden encounter for all parties concerned.

We all have special relationships, no matter how spiritual or how detached from the mundane we believe ourselves to be. In fact, the more detached from the things of the world, the more subtle the special relationships become. There is a Hindu teaching that says that the last thing from which the student must become detached is the desire for detachment. If we had no special relationships, we would not be trapped in the desert. Besides our relationships with our bodies and our parents, our life is filled with an endless supply of special relationships with siblings, friends, teachers, coaches, spouses, children, lovers, enemies, neighbours, bosses and competitors. Special relationships are not limited to people and can include pets, objects, places, ideologies, political and religious views, food, alcohol, drugs, control, power, money, cars, hobbies, work, shopping and emotions to which we cling such as suffering, pain and obsessions of all kinds. Make a list of those things you can't live without, and there you have your very own special relationships. A relationship becomes special when our happiness depends on it being a certain way, when having or living with the object of our desire is better than living without it.

> The ego wishes no one well. Yet its survival depends on your belief that you are exempt from its evil intentions. It counsels, therefore, that if you are host to it, it will enable you to direct its anger outward, thus protecting you. And thus it embarks on an endless, unrewarding chain of special relationships, forged out of anger and dedicated to but one insane belief; that the more anger you invest outside yourself, the safer you become. (T-15.VII.4:3–6)

Special relationships are of the ego because they are founded on judgment, a reflection of the initial judgment that says that the Son of God was better off separate, without the Father. They serve the very important function of providing handy targets onto which we can project our unwanted guilt. Special relationships can appear to express love as well as hate, disgust, condescension, loathing or variations thereof. Everyone has a favourite singer, actor or politician that they love to hate. The instant they appear on television, you snap to attention and something mean or unkind instantly shoots out of your mouth. You probably have never met the person, but there they are, the perfect mark for your projections.

Judgment says that one person is more deserving of our love, respect or consideration than another. Anything that carries even a whiff of specialness or differences is of the ego. Only that which is the same is of God. Love cannot be shared between the different. The special love of the ego is shared with a select few and as such cannot be the Love of God, for the Love of God is for everyone, equally. There is no special love in heaven. The special love relationship is the most insidious of all, Jesus tells us, for it is really hatred in disguise. To say that we love someone exclusively is to say that they are special, distinct, not like everyone else. In heaven, where all is one—therefore the same—all are loved equally by God. Special love excludes; it is a very subtle form of attack, essentially an act of hatred. God's Love is all-inclusive; if one is separate from the whole, that one is not deserving of God's Love. The Course teaches that what we see in our brother is a reflection of how we really feel deep down about ourselves. If we judge that our brother is not deserving of God's Love, it is because we have first judged that we are not deserving of that Love. Ultimately, to withhold love from someone is to withhold love from ourselves.

Jesus wants us to see that we are all the same, that we are different parts of the one split mind, but this is not what we see when we look with "eyes that don't see." Our bodies, via our brains, were designed to perceive other bodies and, in particular, to recognize the differences between bodies. No two bodies are alike, and we see this as a marvellous feat of nature, never realizing that it is these differences that keep us from what we ache for the most, the Love of God, for only in sameness can His Love be known. The essential purpose of all special relationships is to separate, to push away the Love of God. The object of our desire becomes a substitute for the true love we seek, the love we have rejected in favour of our experience of separation. In separation, there can be no real love.

A Different Kind of Forgiveness

> Forgiveness recognizes what you thought your brother did to you has not occurred. It does not pardon sins and make them real. It sees there was no sin. And in that view are all your sins forgiven. What is sin, except a false idea about God's Son? Forgiveness merely sees its falsity, and therefore lets it go. What then is free to take its place is now the Will of God. (W-pII.1.1:1–7)

A work on *A Course in Miracles*, even an introductory one such as this, would be incomplete without a discussion of the subject of forgiveness. True, the practice of forgiveness has become an important component of many healing and spiritual practices in recent years. Forgiveness will set you free; forgiveness will heal. Relinquish your grievances and experience peace. This practice has been very helpful for many people, leading to the mending of broken relationships by facilitating the release of anger, resentment and hatred.

It has enabled some people who have suffered heinous crimes to move forward with their lives, without which they may never have pulled themselves out of their pain and agony, while others have even sidestepped self-destructive and suicidal paths.

The seeker wanting to awaken from the dream must take forgiveness one step further. Since *A Course in Miracles* states flatly that there is no world, there is no sin and what we see is a projection of our own thoughts of hatred and fear, it must follow that its definition of forgiveness must be different from the usual definitions. And, of course, it is. Forgiveness, in fact, constitutes the backbone of the teachings of the Course, whereby Jesus asks us to forgive our brother for what he has *not* done.

It took me years to understand what the Course's version of forgiveness actually means, and even longer to figure out how to apply it in my life. At first, I thought I could work my way around the subject, not really seeing much that needed to be forgiven. And when someone did do something—for example, cut me off in traffic causing me to nearly have a heart attack—to say to myself that I should forgive them for what they had *not* done seemed silly. Also, to say that there wasn't really anyone out there, when clearly there was, didn't make much sense either. At first, the whole forgiveness thing didn't really work for me, so, back to the drawing board I went.

The forgiveness of *A Course in Miracles* is not the form of forgiveness with which most of us are familiar. As a Catholic, I was taught to pray for forgiveness from God. I never understood why I should pray for God's forgiveness if He had created us in His image—and logic would dictate that I must have been created sinless since God had to be sinless—but this is what was required of good Catholics. The Course's forgiveness is not about forgiving your brother for taking your bicycle and accidentally riding it into a ditch or forgiving your ex-spouse for breaking your heart by cheating on you or forgiving a parent for having treated you unfairly. Those would be examples of "forgiveness-to-destroy" because they essentially make the error real. The traditional form of forgiveness says that my brother has sinned, that he has sinned against *me*, so I'm innocent, but I forgive him because I'm a good, spiritually evolved, kind-hearted person. Besides which, my forgiveness will buy me a front-row seat in heaven. This kind of forgiveness does not reflect sameness; once again, as it is founded on differences, it must be of the ego. Its purpose is to make the other appear as the victimizer, while I, appearing magnanimous, kind and understanding, remain an innocent victim. We are different; love cannot truly be experienced.

> Forgiveness, on the other hand, is still, and quietly does nothing. It offends no aspect of reality, nor seeks to twist it to appearances it likes. It merely looks, and waits, and judges not. He who would not forgive must judge, for he must justify his failure to forgive. (W-pII.1.4:1–4)

While the special relationship is the ego's weapon of choice for maintaining the illusion of separation, forgiveness is the Holy Spirit's remedy of choice for returning us to our natural condition of wholeness. This new kind of forgiveness is a simple, though slightly more involved process, that is difficult to apply without a solid understanding of the metaphysics of the Course, which provides the necessary framework for its practice. Forgiveness brings illusion to truth, darkness to light, true healing for all concerned.

The ego would have us look with eyes that don't see, the body's eyes; the Holy Spirit would have us look with true vision, untainted by the dark perceptions of judgment and specialness. The physical eyes are trained to see shapes, shades, forms—essentially, differences. The Holy Spirit's vision sees that we are all the same, that we all suffer from the same belief in separation and the resulting pain of having rejected the Love of God. While the ego interprets my brother's actions as attack, competition, criticism, hatred, meanness, unkindness, malice, rudeness, inconsiderateness, the Holy Spirit sees that we are all—each and every one of us—calling for love. Since there are only two ways of looking, it becomes very easy to identify which way of looking at my brother I have chosen.

Forgiveness requires that we be willing to take an honest look at what seems to be happening, to look beyond our judgments and projections, but, most importantly, to do so without judging ourselves. No one is eager to assume full responsibility for their pain or their suffering or to admit that they chose to be unfairly treated. If we experience peace, this is what we wished; if we experience suffering or pain, even though we may claim to seek peace, this too was our desire. This is why Jesus asks us to look without judging ourselves and, more importantly, he asks us to not look alone, but with him or the Holy Spirit. We might have to overlook—look beyond—several layers of our own judgments and projections before we finally reach the point where we see that the person is really like ourselves, fearful, lost and seeking the love we have all thrown away in our choice for separation. Forgiveness requires that we be willing to push aside the dark curtains of illusion until nothing remains but the light of truth, to look at the problem as it is, not as we have set it up.

> Let me realize today that the problem is always some form of grievance that I would cherish. Let me also understand that the solution is always a miracle with which I let the grievance be replaced. Today I would remember the simplicity of salvation by reinforcing the lesson that there is one problem and one solution. The problem is a grievance; the solution is a miracle. And I invite the solution to come to me through my forgiveness of the grievance, and my welcome of the miracle that takes its place. (W-pI.90.1:2–6)

A typical forgiveness process might proceed as follows: first, I recognize that something must have gone wrong because I am no longer at peace. Somewhere along the way, I switched to the wrong-minded thought system of the ego and am now looking through the lens of judgment. Now comes the hard part. No matter what seems to have happened, I acknowledge that my experience is a choice I have made. I chose to be unfairly treated, to be victimized, to be hurt, to be criticized, to become fearful, to be attacked. Then, I stand back from the situation and retreat into my mind, where

I remind myself that everything I perceive and experience in this multi-faceted world of form is an outward picture of my own inner condition. The Son appears to have fragmented into many, and so all of what I see is a consequence of that one thought of separation. What I see outside is something that I believe to be true about myself, something I do not want to keep, something I feel compelled to project outside of my mind.

As I begin to look, I see the person who I believe has caused me to lose my peace as a body that is male or female, young or old, familiar or not—the typical, neutral judgments that we make on a daily basis. Then I pull back into my mind and look beyond the surface, acknowledging those perceptions and judgments that have stirred up the emotions and responses that are upsetting my peace of mind. Perhaps I see the person as threatening, unfriendly, judgmental, foolish, mean, petty, critical. These are the perceptions that keep me riveted to the world of form and maintain the illusion of differences. My interpretations, as seen through the lens of the ego, prove that I am a victim, that I am vulnerable, that something or someone outside is doing something to me, therefore I exist as a separate being. These interpretations serve to validate my choice for separation.

Since what I experience is all of my own doing, meaning that no one can really take the peace of God away from me unless I wish it so, it is also within my power to undo this situation. The Course does not ask that I fix the situation, that I change the person or that I try to make the person see things differently, nor that I analyze the situation. It only asks that I be willing to look at the situation the way I have set it up, acknowledge that this is not the outcome I really want and then be willing to choose to look at it differently, with the lens of the Holy Spirit. This process is about undoing; it is not about doing anything in the world. It is about undoing my incorrect way of looking. When I look with the Holy Spirit, I will see the other person, as myself, calling for love, a child far from his true home, looking for another way of seeing. The rest of the job of removing the darkness, for myself and for the other person, is in the hands of the Holy Spirit. I don't need to do anything more. How sweet is that?

Holy Spirit's Vision

Non-judgment, Defencelessness, Kindness

In his book *Forgiveness and Jesus*, Ken Wapnick tells of how he responded when someone broke into his apartment in the middle of the night. It is a story that has remained in the back of my mind ever since because of its clear and simple expression of the forgiveness process.

Several years ago, I was awakened in the middle of the night by the sudden realization there was someone standing in my room. After the momentary shock, I remembered "there is nothing to fear," and calmly asked my uninvited guest: "What can I do for you?" The situation was not obscure, however. It was clear that the man was on drugs and desperately needed money for his next fix; burglars rarely enter occupied apartments. He threateningly held his hand in his jacket as if he had a gun, to punctuate his demand. My defenselessness seemed to change the atmosphere in the room, however, and the man soon began apologizing for having broken in and disturbing my sleep. I gave him whatever money I had in my wallet, and the man paused as he took it and then returned a couple of dollars, saying: "this is *all* your money; I can't leave you with nothing." And he went on apologizing. I assured him it was all right, and urged him to do what he had to do. As I ushered the man to the hall, waiting with him for the elevator, I said: "God bless you." His final words as he disappeared into the elevator were: "Please pray for me." I assured him I would, although I knew that this holy encounter had *been* the prayer. No injustice had been done, for there had been no real loss. The amount of money was small "price" indeed for the blessing of forgiveness that had been given and received as one.[1]

I was deeply moved by this story, in particular, by how well it portrays the breadth of this forgiveness practice. Not only is the person who is practising forgiveness healed, forgiveness also extends to the other person. All the more reason to forgive our brothers for what they have not done; only then can true healing occur.

Releasing the Past

I was vacuuming the basement, the laundry room, workshop room, yoga room, avidly, if not obsessively, seeking out every little speck of dirt I could find. Karma yoga, I called it. It was my symbolic way of cleaning out the dirt I feel inside. I had been looking at my dark feelings toward my mom for several months, and I had, as yet, not been successful in releasing much of the deep feelings of resentment. I knew that the Course does not ask us to change our feelings, only to acknowledge them and to let the forgiveness process take its course. But I had reached a point where I was really tired of the darkness, and I told Jesus that I felt that something would have to give. Our situation could not continue as it had. I wanted my mom to be happy, to be peaceful. I wanted to be rid of the darkness that stood between us and the Love of God.

> You consider it "natural" to use your past experience as the reference point from which to judge the present. Yet this is *unnatural* because it is delusional. When you have learned to look on everyone with no reference at all to the past, either his or yours as you perceived it, you will be able to learn from what you see *now*. For the past can cast no shadow to darken the present, *unless you are afraid of light*. And only if you are would you choose to bring darkness with you, and by holding it in your mind, see it as a dark cloud that shrouds your brothers and conceals their reality from your sight. (T-13.VI.2:1–5)

---

1. Kenneth Wapnick, *Forgiveness and Jesus*, page 90.

I moved the television cabinet away from the wall and attacked the dust bunnies that had accumulated between the wires. I was cleaning the house, attacking the dirt, just like my mother did. Only, I was using the vacuum cleaner; she used a cloth floor mop. Then I thought about how I disliked how she cleaned the house. It didn't matter what she cleaned; I somehow found something to dislike about it. The dishes, the floor, the wine bottles, it didn't matter. Then I recalled how, when I was a child, I felt that she had placed house-keeping duties between her and me. Cleaning was more important than playing with me. I do not recall my mom ever playing with me. She was always too busy cleaning something. She was the consummate homemaker. The needy child in me believed that she loved her housework more than she loved me.

I then extrapolated this line of thought to incorporate what I had learned from the Course. My mom, as the principle authority figure in my childhood, was a symbol of God. She put housework before me, just like God put his special godly work before me. Neither had time for me; neither loved me. I resented my mom because she had not indulged my specialness, like God had not recognized my specialness. In her own wisdom, she had taught me to be independent and very self-reliant—traits that would serve my ego's script very well in the world of form, traits that led me to keep love away, a reflection of my fear of the Love of God.

I suddenly just laughed. It was all so incredibly silly. I laughed, but I also wanted to cry, all at once, yet I felt no sadness, only profound and total release. The whole thing was so incredibly childish. I put down my vacuum cleaner and went to find my mom. It was time to go for a walk, enjoy the sunshine. I had spent my adult life putting my work between myself and others; I did the same thing while my mom lived with me. Work was my buffer, keeping us apart. It was time for healing; I was no longer a prisoner of my past. I felt tremendous relief as the darkness of years of resentment was replaced by the light of forgiveness, preparing the way for the expression of love.

My mom was on the phone in her office, but I couldn't wait to invite her to go for that walk. There was no need to talk about anything; rehashing the past was not necessary. Moving forward in a forgiveness framework would take care of the healing. There was no past; only the decision in the present to make a different choice. I did a little jig and caught her attention. "Feel like going for a walk?" I asked. To which she replied, without hesitation, that she would love to, and would soon be off the phone. She joined me while I had a quick bowl of soup, and asked if I had any empty boxes. Not sure what she meant, I asked, "What for?" To which she replied that she would be moving in with my brother the following week; he had a room all ready for her. He had recently separated from his wife, and was eager to share his large home with our mom. She was now free to move on to the next leg of her journey, and I on to mine. Although I understood this to be only the beginning of our healing, I felt that it was a very good beginning.

> The secret of salvation is but this: that you are doing this unto yourself. No matter what the form of the attack, this still is true. Whoever takes the role of enemy and of attacker, still is this the truth. Whatever seems to be the cause of any pain and suffering you feel, this is still true. For you would not react at all to figures in a dream you knew that you were dreaming. Let them be as hateful and as vicious as they may, they could have no effect on you unless you failed to recognize it is your dream. (T-27.VIII.10:1–6)

All My Brothers Are Special

If we desire the peace of God, we must learn to look at our brothers without judgment. The Course explains quite clearly that judgment comes from looking through the lens of the ego and that its purpose is to maintain separation. Jesus asks us to choose to look at our brothers with the Holy Spirit, through the lens of non-judgment. Since this is a choice, the ego's, or the Holy Spirit's way of looking, it then follows clearly that whatever happens will reflect that choice.

We remain always responsible for our experience. If I feel unfairly treated or attacked or wronged by someone, it is because I have chosen to judge their behaviour as other than the call for love that it is. How can anything we do here, in this place that is not our true home, believing ourselves to be cut off from the love of our Father, be anything *but* a call for love?

Differences imply that I exist as a separate being. When we look at our brothers, since we are all part of the same split mind, we are really looking at a mirror of ourselves. If we see fear, it is our fear; if we see love, it is our love. If we forgive our brothers for what they have not done, we forgive ourselves for what we have not done. If I have chosen the lens of judgment, it is so that I can borrow my innocence at someone else's expense. They are guilty for having caused me to be upset or to lose my peace. It is their fault, not mine.

Judgment always implies differences; the ego needs for there to be differences so that guilt can be projected outside my mind. How could I accuse someone of being guilty if I saw them as myself? Racial, social, class or any other kind of prejudice is an overt expression of this need for convenient scapegoats for the projection of our guilt and self-hatred. The Course says that we are all the same, but we say that no, some are more worthy of my love than others, while some are even deserving of my hatred and loathing. Since the Love of God is all-inclusive, love that excludes cannot be real love.

Jesus does not expect us to go out and form loving relationships with everyone we meet. First of all, we do not even know what real love is. Then, to go out and forge relationships with everyone on the planet would be silly, and the Course is anything but silly. Jesus knows well that we have plenty of relationships in our own lives with which to practise our lessons; in fact, we have just the right relationships to practise forgiveness. The Course never tells us what to do in the world. We are simply asked to not exclude anyone from true vision. No matter how hateful or how cruel or how insane they may be, we are asked to look beyond the differences until we see that we are all the same. Free from judgment, we will be in a better position to listen to, and hear, the Holy Spirit's guidance, indicating to us what it is that we need to do or not do. When guided by the Holy Spirit, our actions then will be helpful, kind and loving.

Jesus asks us to overlook—to look beyond—our differences. If we find ourselves unwilling to see without judgment, we are asked to look at our desire to judge, without judgment, and then to observe the resulting feelings of guilt and lack of peace. The Course teaches that, in time, we will see that the price we pay for looking through the lens of the ego is too steep, and we will grow tired of our hatred and our judgments and, especially, of holding love at arm's length. Growing stronger in our desire for the peace of God, we will be more vigilant with our self-observations, perhaps catching ourselves a little sooner, just before we make a judgment. At this point, we know that the teachings of A Course in Miracles have begun to take hold, and the journey to healing has begun in earnest.

That summer, I attended a family barbecue at my brother's house. With little in the way of common interests with my family, I generally did not relish these events, but I recognized these feelings as reflective of my all-pervasive hold on my separateness. As I watched and listened to the usual discussions, arguments, jokes and commentary, a strange feeling came over me, a sort of peaceful, joyful, loving detachment. Late into the night, I had difficulty falling asleep, and so I looked over the day's events with Jesus. I needed to find my bearings. I saw clearly how, in the world of form, nothing really changes, nothing likely ever will change, and whether or not things change does not really matter. It is only my way of looking that can change, and it appeared that on that day, my way of looking had changed.

All of a sudden, I saw everyone who had been sitting outside, around the table and by the pool not as my brothers and mother and friends and family, but I saw everyone, all of us, as fragmented parts of the Sonship, desperately trying to be heard, to be made special, to be distinct, all trying to hold onto the experience of separateness, all seeking to reclaim the thing we want most, the Love of God. In that moment, I saw clearly how we were all the same, each of us sharing in the same insane illusion of separation.

In that moment, the people with whom I had shared a lovely day, with whom I had shared a lifetime of experiences, ceased to be family. Instead, I saw that we were all one Sonship, and as the tears flowed, I felt long-held grievances and resentments and memories flow out of me, with a deep certainty of knowing that just beyond, the Love of God awaited.

> You have no idea of the tremendous release and deep peace that comes from meeting yourself and your brothers totally without judgment. When you recognize what you are and what your brothers are, you will realize that judging them in any way is without meaning. In fact, their meaning is lost to you precisely because you are judging them. All uncertainty comes from the belief that you are under the coercion of judgment. You do not need judgment to organize your life, and you certainly do not need it to organize yourself. In the presence of knowledge all judgment is automatically suspended, and this is the process that enables recognition to replace perception. (T-3.VI.3:1–6)

Chapter 9

THE TREACHERY OF SPECIALNESS

The special ones are all asleep, surrounded by a world of loveliness they do not see. Freedom and peace and joy stand there, beside the bier on which they sleep, and call them to come forth and waken from their dream of death. Yet they hear nothing. They are lost in dreams of specialness. (T-24. III.7:1–4)

The Modern-day Cult of Specialness

THE WORLD MAY APPEAR to be growing smaller as we develop more and more increasingly sophisticated communications devices, but parallel to this seeming experience of connectedness, as individuals, we may actually be growing further apart. We live in a time when specialness, uniqueness and differentness have been elevated almost to the rank of spiritual attainment. Find your true self, seek what makes you different, be a "purple cow," celebrate your uniqueness, stand out from the crowd… these are the rallying cries of our coaches and those who would teach us the way to happiness and success. We are urged to create a unique "elevator pitch" to promote ourselves, a strong brand for our products and services, a web presence that is a cut above the competition. There are special needs schools for our children, special needs centres for the grown-ups who don't quite fit in and special services tailored to the unique needs of the elderly. Our phones have distinctive ring tones and faceplates, our desktops are personalized with the images of our experiences and we make up funny names for our blogs and Internet profiles. Restaurants have special menus for those with special dietary needs, heart problems, cholesterol, obesity and diabetes. For those who are healthy, there are vegan, vegetarian and kosher menus. In fact, we can just about personalize any major purchase today, from the options we choose for our cars to the design and finishing of our homes. Our children are raised to express their uniqueness through their dress, speech, actions and special requirements of all sorts, from dietary to environmental.

When I went to school, we wore uniforms, stood in line two-by-two from shortest to tallest, followed the same schedules and study plans, and wrote the same exams. To impose this kind of regulation today would no doubt cause an uproar among our youth—and some parents—who would declare that basic human rights of self-expression had been unfairly trampled on. Yet, no matter how unique we appear to be, we are essentially all the same in our desire to be different.

If anything, given the unique and unusual direction that my life took despite my conventional upbringing, I can be counted among the poster children for specialness. The journey of my life has been rife with uniqueness, something I have willingly embraced and sought after, preferring to define myself by my differences rather than my commonality with others, even preferring solitude over companionship. In fifteen years of business networking, I never once met another astrologer. In fact, even as an astrologer, I avoided all New Age groups and activities. Instead, I put on a suit and brought my unusual craft to the mainstream marketplace. All of these choices served to sustain my specialness. All of these choices served to reinforce the ego's perception of a distinct, separated individual. Yet, what has been the cost, to me, of so much indulgence in specialness?

From the perspective of *A Course in Miracles*, specialness can only lead to anything but peace and happiness. All forms of specialness are of the ego, evidence of the original thought of separation, proof that it is possible to be distinct and separate from perfect oneness. The more we are defined by our specialness, the stronger is our hold on the thought of separation, the greater is our need to defend and maintain this condition. If it is what keeps us from our true wholeness, how then can specialness lead to anything but lack, scarcity and a lifetime spent in its protection? How can specialness lead to that elusive happiness we all seek in this world of illusions and insanity? If only oneness is true, specialness, which serves to maintain separation, must be part of the illusion, part of the dream. What tremendous force must be required to maintain such an unreal and unnatural condition. Yet, for the sake of maintaining our illusory state of separation, we do everything in our power to nurture, foster, protect and cater to our precious specialness.

> You are not special. If you think you are, and would defend your specialness against the truth of what you really are, how can you know the truth? What answer that the Holy Spirit gives can reach you, when it is your specialness to which you listen, and which asks and answers? (T-24.II.4:1–3)

Fall from Grace

It had been a busy few weeks with lots of consults, and any remaining waking hours were spent toggling between the writing, editing and laying out of this book. Although there was still much work to be done, varying the tasks made the job more interesting and kept my mind fresh for the writing. Since I cannot make myself write when I have nothing to say, on those days when words didn't come, I focused on editing and layout. Despite the fact that I had been eager to undertake this writing project when I first began it in early 2009, a year and a half into it I had begun to feel that I had less and less to say, and, even more importantly, that my words seemed to have less and less value. Having understood that writing was one of those "important" activities that kept me rooted in the world, albeit one of my favourite activities, I came to the conclusion that I did not need to write this book and at any time I could simply quit.

Besides which my body would appreciate the break from far too many hours spent at the computer.

Putting occasional doubts aside, I continued with the work and trusted that it would go where it needed to go. Moreover, it seemed that each time I thought of abandoning the writing, something would draw me back into it, like an email from a reader of *Making Peace with God* thanking me for having written my book. People were enjoying my writing; it seemed to have a purpose outside my own healing. Then there was Mike from our Course study group who had mentioned on more than one occasion that I should write something on specialness. I told him that I had it covered, but so far, the subject had only been defined intellectually. It would be helpful to have a real-life example, I thought, and as very often happens with thoughts, almost as soon as they are expressed, so are their consequences. This time, though, I believe I was unprepared for the intensity of the real-life experience.

Parallel to my busy outer life, I was beginning to sense that a shift was taking place deep inside, as though life as I had known it all these years was slowing down, bit by bit, fading into nothing-ness.[1] I had taken to listening to a genre of music that years ago I never thought I would have enjoyed. Jazz and bossa nova were set aside while for hours on end I surrounded myself with the enchant-ing strains of yoga and meditation music, a mix of sacred chants from India and the Orient. During quiet moments, I had begun to experience an almost euphoric sense of deep peace and surrender, and it occurred to me that perhaps the peace of God may not be as far away as I believed it to be.

My growing understanding of the Course had helped me to relinquish many ancient grievances and I was pleased with my progress in the practice of forgiveness. I had grown quite familiar with my ego script, and it was becoming much easier to distinguish between my right- and wrong-minded thinking. At times, I was

---

1. For readers of *The Power of Time*, note that I was deep in the middle of a number 7 Personal Year.

able to catch my ego in action and consciously flip the switch to the right mind, saving myself from much unwanted conflict and distress, very often bringing quick and simple resolution to situations that might have taken much longer to resolve. The chains of the thought system of the ego were being loosened, and the reward was a life of growing serenity and simplicity.

From my shifting perspective, I could see that the desert was shrinking and my oasis was losing much of its significance. There were fewer and fewer things of this world that mattered. In fact, I realized that nothing much of this world really mattered anymore. I was becoming more patient, even making full stops when driving the car. Well, at least most of the time. There was no longer any rush. Where was there to go? What was so important?

More and more, I longed for only one thing, the peace of God. There were moments of extreme contentment, when I felt as though something inside might burst, I would catch my breath, then tears would come. These were not tears of sadness; they were tears of intense inner longing for something I had sought for so long, for something I felt was within reach, something for which I knew I was not yet quite ready. This was, if anything, a rather peculiar state, which I came to refer to as "grace." In those moments, I would willingly have let go of every last thing I held dear, a thought that sent waves of deep release through every fibre of my being.

When working with clients or visiting with family or friends, no matter how nice things appeared on the surface, I saw their pains, their struggles and their yearnings as like my own. I understood that we are all cut from the same cloth; that we all suffer from the same insane thought of separation, from the same longing to return home to our Father. Once, while out running errands, I saw a stranger walking in the opposite direction across the street, and I thought, with great knowing, he is me! This condition continued over several weeks, with the moments of peaceful revelry growing longer each time. Consults began to wane, and I found myself more and more alone, choosing to be alone, welcoming seclusion, a situation that might have caused me serious concern had I any desires for this world. It seemed that during those passing moments of peace and contentment, nothing else mattered.

> Now comes "a period of settling down." This is a quiet time, in which the teacher of God rests a while in reasonable peace. Now he consolidates his learning. Now he begins to see the transfer value of what he has learned. Its potential is literally staggering.... The teacher of God needs this period of respite. He has not yet come as far as he thinks. (M-4.I.6:1–5; 9–10)

Wanting nothing more than to remain in this blissful state, between consults I created the environment that seemed to support it, the music, long periods of silence, quiet meditation, simpler foods, abstinence from wine. Yet, despite my state of enchantment, I remained sufficiently aware of the potential dangers lurking not far afield; at some point, out of fear for its very survival, the ego was bound to rear its ugly mug! While clinging to this mellow mood, I knew enough to not take these experiences to mean more than they were: a temporary excursion into what might be when all the spots of darkness have been brought to the light. This was not yet a permanent condition and I was not surprised when little red flags began to spring up, intruding on my state of grace.

A little voice inside started to taunt me, pointing out that I had not yet gone far enough, that I was not a holy person like Ramana Maharshi, Brother Lawrence or Thomas Merton. It reminded me that my fabricated monkly seclusion was a sure sign that I knew that my peace was fragile and could be taken away from me at the first sign of conflict, and therefore was not the true peace of God. Isolation from the world would only serve the purposes of the ego, shielding me from seeing my projections, preventing me from seeing what I truly believed about myself. It started to look as though the ego had managed to sink its claws into my precious peace. Fortunately, given my otherwise busy and active lifestyle, it was never long before it was necessary for me to interact with others. I knew well that had I moved to a cave in Tibet, I might have missed out on many important learning opportunities. In isolation,

I would not have met the ego where it stood between me and the way out of the desert.

EGO'S PERCEPTION

JUDGMENT, SPECIALNESS, ATTACK!

A client had called a couple of times with questions concerning a publishing dilemma with which she had become entangled. Sharon had written a novel about the search for truth that she strongly felt needed to be shared with the world. Being that the work was in the spiritual genre, she wanted the business dealings with her partner to be just as spiritual. However, there were financial, copyright, ethical, ownership and legal issues at play and clearly the situation had become anything but spiritual. I pointed out that she was attempting to resolve a business matter from a spiritual perspective, and that she might consider separating the two. She was clearly passionate about her work, and since I wanted to be helpful, we agreed to meet.

> Comparison must be an ego device, for love makes none. Specialness always makes comparisons.... Pursuit of specialness is always at the cost of peace.... Never can there be peace among the different. (T.24.II.1:1–2; 2:1; I.9:7)

However, as the day approached, a mild disquiet began to stir in the back of my mind, pushing clouds of darkness dangerously close to my oasis of contentment. One of the issues that concerned me was that Sharon might ask me to read her manuscript. I tried to push these disturbing thoughts aside, but the truth of the matter was that I really did not want to read it. She had already outlined the story for me months earlier and I had judged it as somewhat naive. Nor was it reflective of the teachings of *A Course in Miracles*, which I had judged to be superior on the spiritual hierarchy. Clearly, I had grabbed the ego's lens of judgment.

In the end, our meeting was brief. We both had appointments that afternoon and our time was limited, but we did get a chance to discuss the publishing process. As it turned out, Sharon just wanted to show me her manuscript; she did not ask me to read it. Her enthusiasm for her book was evident and she truly believed it to be an important spiritual work. Our encounter was pleasant and harmonious. In fact, no one would have known that a storm was brewing deep inside me, one that would completely obliterate the deep peace I had recently stumbled upon.

After Sharon left my office, I thought about my growing sense of uneasiness. Then it dawned on me with shocking clarity that what was really bothering me was my deep annoyance with her ingenuous display of specialness and what it truly represented. Her story was special; she was special. She was not even a student of the Course and she was writing on spirituality. Nor had she read my book, imagine that! She was only concerned with her story.

With each interaction that followed over the next few days, specialness themes exploded. I saw nothing but specialness scripts everywhere I turned. Everyone was suffering in a special way; everyone had something special to say; everyone had something special to do; everyone had a special problem; everyone had a special gift; everyone had a special place to go; everyone had something special that needed to be acknowledged. Everyone had something special to tell me, to show me, to take from me. Specialness, specialness, specialness. Specialness ruled the world! Specialness kept the world divided. Specialness kept oneness away. Specialness kept the Love of God away.

> Specialness is the function that you gave yourself. It stands for you alone, as self-created, self-maintained, in need of nothing, and unjoined with anything beyond the body. In its eyes you are a separate universe, with all the power to hold itself complete within itself, with every entry shut against intrusion, and every window barred against the light. Always attacked

and always furious, with anger always fully justified, you have pursued this goal with vigilance you never thought to yield, and effort that you never thought to cease. And all this grim determination was for this; you wanted specialness to be the truth. (T-24.VI.11:1–5)

A dense cloud of anger, hatred and resentment swooped down like a North Atlantic fog, pouring itself thickly onto the fragile coastline of my fledgling state of grace. It wasn't long before I realized what was happening. Recalling that since the world I see is an outside picture of an inward condition, what I was perceiving in others was my own specialness. Boom. A dark, dense wall of desolation dropped around the oasis of my specialness while the desert rolled out forever before me. I felt trapped. Evil. Guilty. Sinful. If anything, I was most deserving of punishment. In my eagerness to hold onto my peaceful state, I had stirred up tremendous fear in my ego and, as a result, had come face-to-face with the darkness of my own specialness. My practice, my writing, my public profile, my work with the Course—all these aspects of my life reeked of specialness and I wanted to banish them all. These were symbols of the guilt that resulted from my decision for separation, reminders of my choice against God, all things that kept away the peace of God. I felt great loathing for this person so completely steeped in specialness. I wanted to eradicate the specialness, stomp it out, kill it. My specialness had destroyed the peace of God. It had added miles and miles to the desert of my journey. It had cost me my precious state of grace.

As I sank into the abyss of my dark realization, I saw that the self I knew as Pauline Edward and all the things that I believed to be so important, all the things with which I identified, all of it, all of them, belonged to the desert. In leaving the desert, what was it then that would remain? Serious doubt arose. Jesus promises us that we are abandoning something of no value for something of far greater value—the everything of heaven. But was that really true? How was I to know for sure? Since this was a course in mind training, how did I know I wasn't just deluding myself? What if I was being brainwashed by some insane teaching? How would I know?

> You have built your whole insane belief system because you think you would be helpless in God's Presence, and you would save yourself from His Love because you think it would crush you into nothingness. You are afraid it would sweep you away from yourself and make you little, because you believe that magnitude lies in defiance, and that attack is grandeur. You think you have made a world God would destroy; and by loving Him, which you do, you would throw this world away, which you *would*. Therefore, you have used the world to cover your love, and the deeper you go into the blackness of the ego's foundation, the closer you come to the Love that is hidden there. *And it is this that frightens you.* (T-13.III.4:1–5)

Indeed, I had fallen into a wretchedly dark place, worse than any previous depression, because this time there was no turning back, for the oasis held no appeal. There was nowhere to turn for comfort, other than in my mind, that same mind that had shown me a dark side of myself that I only wanted to turn away from. What now? Seeing no way out, for about a second and a half, I nearly regretted having gone down this road with Jesus and his Course. I was beginning to think that this path might not be for me. Perhaps I knew what it said intellectually, but living it was a whole other matter. Maybe I just wasn't spiritual enough for *A Course in Miracles*. I was doomed to experience the semblance of life in a lifeless desert. This was worse than death; this was like being dead and knowing I was dead. This darkness was not black, for that would have held mystery, a hidden promise. This darkness was grey. Nor was there even the hint of light. The grey darkness held only the desolation of nothingness.

Concluding that I was way over my head with this spiritual path, I decided then and there that I would stop all Course-related activities, starting with the writing of this book, for clearly I knew nothing, at least nothing that deserved being written about. I would retrieve the two chapters that Mike was proofreading and there would be no more. Next, I would disband our Course study group; we were a very small group, surely no one would miss it. How could I continue to host a study group for a spirituality that was not for me? Instead, I would focus all my attention and energies on consults and workshops. I had given this path all I had and, in the end, I had failed.

Despite my valiant attempts to move on and get my old life back, the darkness remained. Each morning that followed greeted me with the dark despair of the desert that would be host to the remainder of my life. My old life wasn't coming back, and my discouragement grew. I felt as though something inside had died. Consults picked up again, slowly, and I tried my best to focus on the business of normal life. In an attempt to understand what I was experiencing, I leafed through some books I had read decades earlier and finally settled in the garden one afternoon with an iced tea and Arthur Osborne's *Ramana Maharshi and the Path of Self-Knowledge*. Immediately, I was stunned at how close Ramana's teaching of Self-enquiry was to *A Course in Miracles*, but most of all, I was stunned to find that, contrary to when I had first read these books over thirty-five years earlier, now I actually understood what they said. Like Jesus, Ramana stressed the importance of being vigilant for the mind, of sorting out the valuable from the valueless, of knowing which questions really mattered. Like Jesus, Ramana taught of the importance of trusting one's teacher.

> Through this despair you travel now, yet it is but illusion of despair. The death of specialness is not your death, but your awaking into life eternal. You but emerge from an illusion of what you are to the acceptance of yourself as God created you. (T-24.II.14:3–5)

Sharing the Journey with the Holy Spirit

It appears that it would take more than a desolation darker than death before my faith in the Course was entirely extinguished. Though perhaps not holy, my inherently persistent nature would not allow me to quit quite yet. In search of comfort and clarity, I decided to go for a long walk with my MP3 player loaded up with one of my favourite Ken Wapnick workshops,[2] "The Experience of *A Course in Miracles.*" I needed to know what I was doing wrong. Over the next couple of days, clarity returned in little flashes as I began to see the error that was at the root of my difficulty with the Course. I had been managing the journey on my own, without Jesus. There was an "I" that was studying a spiritual system that was designed to teach that there is no "I." Clearly, I had not been looking with Jesus by my side, nor with the Holy Spirit. In just about everything I did, I had been looking through the lens of the ego, and therefore would remain limited in my application of the teachings of the Course. If I wanted to see the truth, if I wanted to see the way out of the desert, I would have to look with eyes that can truly see that far.

I will step back and let him lead the way. (W-pI.155)

As a first step, I acknowledged that I needed to place more trust in the Holy Spirit and in Jesus. But, the ego quickly chimed in, how could I manage such a seemingly impossible feat? I was a practical, hands-on kind of person, this was a course in mind training and, right now, my mind was not showing me much light. How could I trust that I could ever learn to see with the right mind? It was all so intangible and abstract, all so frightening and so bleak. There was only darkness in my mind, and I was afraid that the light would remain forever out of my reach. Worst of all, I was afraid that I would never again feel the enchanting state of grace that had so shamefully slipped out of my reach.

In a way, it was a good thing that the answers were not forth-coming in the world outside my mind simply because *A Course in Miracles* is a course in mind training, designed to empower its students with the tools to make a different choice. If answers had

---

2. Actually, there is no hierarchy of workshops—I like them all. I felt this one would be appropriate for my current state of mind. I later gleaned additional insights from "Escape from Love: Dissociating *A Course in Miracles*", and still more from "The Real World."

come from the world of form, since the world is the ego's solution to the problem of guilt, I might have received answers that suited the ego's plan to keep me in the desert. That being the case, then I surely would never have found true hope. I needed to go to the place that was the cause, the source of my distress, the mind's decision for the ego's thought system of separation. To look with the Holy Spirit meant that I needed to see that there was an alternative to the thought system of separation. To look with the Holy Spirit meant that I needed to accept to see my brother sinless and, above all, to accept to see myself as sinless. This I had forgotten to do when I had seen the other through the eyes of judgment. In looking through the lens of the ego, I had seen specialness; had I looked through the lens of the Holy Spirit, I would have seen the call for love that was clearly there.

Still engulfed in darkness, though more conscious of remembering to keep the Holy Spirit by my side, I felt guided to send Mike an email to set up a meeting so I could pick up the chapters he had proofread. I proposed ice cream at an outdoor ice cream stand nearby that I knew had diabetic-friendly treats. He eagerly accepted. The plan was to simply go over the edits, which I would then take home, and that would be the end of that. There was no need to tell him of my decision to stop writing, nor of my decision to cancel the study group meetings. The next two Thursdays conveniently fell on legal holidays giving us a couple of weeks off anyways. I could reasonably declare a break for the summer period; the fall session would be another matter. I would wait and see. In my email, I told him that I would be at his door at one o'clock on the appointed day, barring a major snowstorm, meaning, that since it was the middle of June, I would be there. Not wanting to drag him into my pit of despair, I decided that I would keep the conversation light and positive.

The weather was uncertain on the day of our meeting, so I threw a raincoat and umbrella in the back seat of the car, just in case. It had been nearly a week since my fall from grace, and although I had been somewhat concerned that I might not be good company, when Mike and I sat on the bench to eat our iced treats—a sugar-free strawberry sherbet for him and a butterscotch sundae for me—I realized that I did not need to worry about what to say or what to do. The Holy Spirit would be with us. Mike is a wonderful poet, and he shared a poem that reflected rather well my own struggle with darkness. As we chatted, I grew comfortable enough to relate my experiences of the past couple of weeks, which I did with great flourish. In his wisdom, he reminded me that where there was darkness, the light was not too far away.

I'm not sure how it all got started, but at some point, we began to laugh. I shared with him that I had understood that I knew nothing, the actual words were: "I don't know shit," to which he responded that someone had written a book on that subject. We laughed heartily as we tried to find analogies for darker than the darkest night, we joked about our inherent belief in our evil, dark, sinful natures and the ingenious ways our egos express resistance to the Course's message. As we laughed, any remaining wisps of darkness disappeared and nothing else mattered. I told him that I had learned a very important lesson, which was to take the journey very, very slowly.

When I returned home, I placed the chapters Mike had read next to my computer to insert the edits he had recommended. As for the writing, I decided to let things come, as they were meant. I had received two emails that week from readers of *Making Peace with God*. Although I had no idea if they, or anyone, had need of another book, I placed the entire matter in the hands of the Holy Spirit. I also felt that the Holy Spirit had guided Mike and I to spend that wonderful happy carefree hour and a half together, for which I was very grateful. The world could have fallen down around us, and we would not even have noticed. In fact, we were laughing so heartily that we were not aware of the minor quake[3] that hit the

---

3. On June 23, 2010 at 1:41 p.m., a minor earthquake hit the Ontario–Quebec border.

region while we were feasting on ice cream, Course talk and the joy of shared vision.

Joining with Him in seeing is the way in which you learn to share with Him the interpretation of perception that leads to knowledge. You cannot see alone. Sharing perception with Him Whom God has given you teaches you how to recognize what you see. It is the recognition that nothing you see means anything alone. Seeing with Him will show you that all meaning, including yours, comes not from double vision, but from the gentle fusing of everything into *one* meaning, *one* emotion and *one* purpose. God has one purpose which He shares with you. The single vision which the Holy Spirit offers you will bring this oneness to your mind with clarity and brightness so intense you could not wish, for all the world, not to accept what God would have you have. Behold your will, accepting it as His, with all His Love as yours. All honor to you through Him, and through Him unto God. (T-14.VII.7:1–9)

Chapter 10

THE HAPPY LEARNER

You who have played that you are lost to hope, abandoned by your Father, left alone in terror in a fearful world made mad by sin and guilt; be happy now. That game is over. Now a quiet time has come, in which we put away the toys of guilt, and lock our quaint and childish thoughts of sin forever from the pure and holy minds of Heaven's children and the Son of God. (W-pI.153.13:1–3)

A New Beginning

*I*N THE END, MY fall from grace was little more than a slight stumble along the most significant journey of my life, a deeply humbling experience, but one that gave me a whole new respect for the power of the Course's teaching. *A Course in Miracles* has allowed me to see that it is actually possible for a non-holy person to return home, eventually. Since there was no doubt that I truly wanted this goal, a little fall from grace would not stop me in my pursuit. Once again, I decided to pay very close attention to the teaching Jesus gave us. It was a choice; it was my decision, and as my faith in the process was revived, life slowly returned to normal. And yes, as the days passed, the exquisite moments of grace returned, only now they came in more manageable doses, little hints of what was yet to come when all spots of darkness would be removed, a sense of wholeness and peace that was not of the desert, no matter how lovely was my oasis.

Although this book was written as part of my healing process, never did I expect to be taken on such a deep and intense journey. Jesus meant business when he gave us *A Course in Miracles*. We asked for a better way, and he gave us one. Actually, he went one step further by giving us the tools that would help us leave our make-believe lives in the desert: he gave us a true miracle. As his students, I am sure we have given him—and will continue to give him—cause to shake his head and forgive us now and then, for, you see, we don't even recognize that the desert is not our real home. We think we can dress up our little oasis, make it look good and everything will be fine. But Jesus is a patient teacher. He has to be. I am certain he was aware, right from the start, that his bold new teaching was not what we had in mind when we asked for help and that we would have a lot of difficulty accepting it, let alone applying it in our lives. It certainly was not what I had ever expected, nor even imagined possible. Clearly, we wanted, and desperately needed, help to fix our troubled oases, but I doubt that many of us had considered actually *leaving* the desert as an option.

> The journey to God is merely the reawakening of the knowledge of where you are always, and what you are forever. It is a journey without distance to a goal that has never changed. (T-8.VI.9:6–7)

As I reached the final pages of this manuscript, it became clear, once more, that what would follow was yet another new beginning, and I felt well equipped to embark on the next leg of my journey home. What was learned needed to be applied every minute of every day. I think the first step in working with the Course was to be convinced that it was the right path for me; then I needed to know that I could actually understand it enough to apply it in my life. It was only once I began to apply this teaching in earnest that I could appreciate its tremendous power and effectiveness. Jesus wants us to learn a new way of looking; the Course is designed to teach just that. Though I continue to listen to Ken Wapnick workshops and read the big book with the navy blue cover, it is in the daily application of the teaching that real learning takes place. True knowledge comes from experience.

The Shrinking World

When I was young, I used to picture the universe as this great big place in which I lived, a place filled with light and life and all manner of people and things and places to explore and discover, so vast that I would experience only a tiny speck of it in the whole of my life. God, Who had made the world, stood beyond the outer limits of our universe. In my mind, that place where God is, at home in Heaven, was far, far away, mysterious and unreachable. That image all changed when, while going for a walk on a beautiful autumn day, I revisited my perception of the world and of God. Suddenly it occurred to me that I had it all backwards. In my mind, I stepped back and thought of the world from the new perspective of *A Course in Miracles*. As I stepped further and further back, the world, in fact, all of what we call our universe, this never-ending cosmos that had once seemed so overwhelmingly vast, began to shrink and fold in on itself, losing all sense of life and light. While darkness replaced what I had long thought the home of my tiny existence, a great bright light began to envelop its external perimeter, closing in on it, further causing the world to shrink. This light, I understood, was of God; the darkness was not of God, the darkness was this world. Whereas in the past I might have found this line of thought, if not frightful, then at the very least disturbing, at that moment, I felt very safe and protected. In fact, I do not recall a time in my life when I felt safer than in that one transcendent moment.

Awakening Holiness

There is no will but God's.
I am at peace.
Nothing can disturb me. My will is God's.
My will and God's are one.
God wills peace for His Son. (W-pI.74.3:5–9)

Many times I have wondered if I could ever reach a point where I would allow my will to be fully aligned with God's. Would I really be able one day to set my ego-driven will aside and let myself feel the deep comfort of knowing that His will is my will? And besides, what was God's Will for me? In the fall of 2009, I read *The Seven Storey Mountain*, the work that had inspired my search for the truth so many years earlier. I am certain now that, had I been a boy, I would have followed in Thomas Merton's footsteps and joined the Trappists, perhaps even at Gethsemani. Many times I wondered how Merton would have responded to *A Course in Miracles*. I don't know why, but it seemed important for me to know what he might have thought of its bold new spiritual perspective. Would the Course have answered his questions? Soothed his unsettled soul? Brought him the peace he sought? It puzzled me that the Church, with its teachings so wildly opposed to those of the Course, could produce such saintly men and women such as Thomas Merton, St. John of the Cross, Padre Pio, Brother Lawrence and Theresa of Avila.

Needing to make peace with the religion of my childhood, I picked up another of Merton's books. It had been well over thirty years since I had read *The Sign of Jonas*, and though I was well past my Catholic mystic phase, something kept pulling me there. Merton had struggled with his desire for a life of peaceful contemplation, finding that Gethsemani was not the tranquil place it should have been. Not uncommon during wartime, the monastery was experiencing an unusual period of rapid growth and expansion and it seemed that there was not enough of the quiet time for contemplation and prayer he so much desired. With memories of my own attraction for such a life and an increasing desire for the peaceful life, I read a passage from the early pages of *The Sign of Jonas*—perhaps the only passage I was meant to read—for it gave me the answers I needed at the time.

In his journal entry for that day, Merton expressed his complete trust in the Love of God, a love that he knew would take care of all aspects of his life. He chided himself for thinking that there could be a more suitable environment for experiencing closeness with his beloved Father, finding himself occasionally annoyed with the distractions and noise of the busy monastery. In the end, he realized that he could enjoy every hour of every day in the presence of God, because God was with him always.

Although the form of Merton's words did not fall within the framework of the language of *A Course in Miracles*, their content came from that place in our minds that we all share, the memory of that which is true, the longing for our true home. What touched me the most was his profound love and desire to be with God. It was total; he had no other desire in his heart. These were the words of a truly holy man. Again, as was the case over thirty years ago, I was struck by his unwavering faith. This time, however, I recognized that my own faith had become firmly rooted. This gave me great strength and the unwavering courage to continue on my journey. Merton's words rang with my own sincere desire to return home and be with God, and as I read, I wept for the truth that stirred deep in my heart.

As another example of one who had accepted to walk on the journey out of the desert, into the Love of God, Brother Lawrence tells of how he would go about his daily tasks by keeping his awareness on the presence of God.

> "The time of business," said he, "does not with me differ from the time of prayer; and in the noise and clatter of my kitchen, while several persons are at the same time calling for different things, I possess God in as great tranquility as if I were upon my knees at the blessed sacrament."[1]

I understand that it does not matter where I am or what I do in the world, just like Merton understood that he could be close to God no matter which monastery he was assigned to, and Brother Lawrence knew that he could be close to God no matter the task at hand. As much as I think I would have given up my practice for the peace and tranquillity of a simple job in a flower shop or

---

1. Brother Lawrence, *The Practice of the Presence of God and the Spiritual Maxims*, page 16.

better yet, as a cook in a monastery, I knew that I was meant to do the work I was doing, and that to long for anything else was only a way of avoiding my true function, my only function. My life is clearly my classroom, perfectly designed for me to learn the lessons of forgiveness that will facilitate my acceptance of the Atonement. Forgiveness can be practised anywhere; that is my true function. This is God's Will for me. In that knowledge, I began to feel the safety and the warmth of what life might be like if I were to completely give myself over to God. This was the life that I was meant to live, the life that contained all the elements that were needed to lead me out of the desert. It was a blessed life, and I offered it up to God.

> O my child, if you knew what God wills for you, your joy would be complete! And what He wills has happened, for it was always true. When the light comes and you have said, "God's Will is mine," you will see such beauty that you will know it is not of you. Out of your joy you will create beauty in His Name, for your joy could no more be contained than His. The bleak little world will vanish into nothingness, and your heart will be so filled with joy that it will leap into Heaven, and into the Presence of God. I cannot tell you what this will be like, for your heart is not ready. Yet I can tell you, and remind you often, that what God wills for Himself He wills for you, and what He wills for you is yours. (T-11.III.3:1–7)

A few months later, I received an insight that helped me to reconcile my conflicted view of the teachings of the Catholic Church. Yes, it was true that much, perhaps most, of its doctrine was born of the ego's thought system, but since we are all of two minds, it was inevitable that some of its teachings—as with all the teachings of the world's religions—would be right-minded. Those men and women who truly sought the truth were able to navigate past the falsehoods to the truth that lies beyond. Mostly, it was their willingness to set their egos aside that allowed them to be led to the truth. What would Thomas Merton have done with *A Course in Miracles*? Perhaps Father Merton had no need of the Course; his heart was already turned toward the Love of God, as it was with Theresa of

Avila, Sri Ramana Maharshi, Brother Lawrence and many others throughout history.

A Practical Spirituality

> We have repeated how little is asked of you to learn this course.... This is the only thing that you need do for vision, happiness, release from pain and the complete escape from sin, all to be given you. Say only this, but mean it with no reservations, for here the power of salvation lies:
> I am responsible for what I see.
> I choose the feelings I experience, and I decide upon the goal I would achieve.
> And everything that seems to happen to me I ask for, and receive as I have asked.
> Deceive yourself no longer that you are helpless in the face of what is done to you. Acknowledge but that you have been mistaken, and all effects of your mistakes will disappear. (T-21. II.1:1; 2:1–7)

To say that the world is an illusion, though metaphysically true, cannot be very helpful for those of us whose thoughts are not always with God. To ask us to be kind, loving and holy when we are motivated by deeply hidden guilt and fear and hard-wired for self-preservation and survival in a world that is not our true home and, furthermore, a world that is an attack on God, would not be any more helpful. To be told to offer our love to God when we are not even aware of our deep fear and hatred of our Father, well, that would not be very helpful either. To be told that we can choose peace at any time, when we do not even know that we want to be rid of it, is no more helpful than to be told to choose with another mind we don't even know exists.

This is why Jesus gave us such a slowly evolving training program, one that includes a comprehensive text that explains how and why we got to where we are, along with a workbook to get us started in applying its message. He knew very well that we would never be able to be kind, loving and peaceful until we were made aware of the fact that the thought system to which we adhere is one of specialness, hatred and judgment, and is incapable of expressing kindness, love and peacefulness. Only then could he begin to work with us—which he does, once we accept to work with him.

Jesus makes all this very simple for us. The cause of the world we see is our decision for separation. Period. That's all. No need to go any further. To accept this premise can save us a lot of time, since we do not need to analyze and study everything that goes on in the world, nor in our lives—only what goes on in our mind. Our life becomes the classroom in which we can learn to become aware of the choices we make in our mind. In fact, this is the best place to apply this teaching, for this is the story that has made our existence in the world seem very real to us. To deny our life would be to reject our primary classroom, a denial that would probably be indicative of a clever defensive ego manoeuvre. Jesus does not ask us to change our life situations; he wants us to change our mind.

HOLY SPIRIT'S VISION

FORGIVENESS, NON-JUDGMENT, ACCEPTANCE

The application of the teachings of *A Course in Miracles* can be summed up in one simple lesson: since, in truth, I am as God created me, but at the core of my experience, I believe that I am a separate self, in a world, in a body, then I must be of split mind. In that case, there are but two alternatives from which to choose: the Holy Spirit's right-minded vision of oneness expressed as forgiveness and the ego's wrong-minded thought system of separation expressed as judgment, specialness, differences or variations of the perception of separation. Anything more complicated than that is likely to be of the ego. There is only one valid judgment: what I see is either an expression of love or a call for love. If I choose to look with the Holy Spirit's right-minded lens of forgiveness, I choose with the part of the mind that will lead to the memory of the truth of our oneness. The choice for forgiveness can but lead to thoughts, acts and responses that reflect shared interests, acceptance, kindness, defencelessness and love.

> If you but knew how much your Father yearns to have you recognize your sinlessness, you would not let His Voice appeal in vain, nor turn away from His replacement for the fearful images and dreams you made. The Holy Spirit understands the means you made, by which you would attain what is forever unattainable. And if you offer them to Him, He will employ the means you made for exile to restore your mind to where it truly is at home. (W-pII.7.3:1–3)

EGO'S PERCEPTION

JUDGMENT, SPECIALNESS, FEAR

If I perceive anything other than an expression of love or a call for love, then I have very likely chosen to look at my brother with the ego's lens of judgment. That being the case, I have projected my own inner darkness onto my brother. It is my decision to hold onto the thought of guilt that hides the love or the call for love that is being expressed. If I choose with the thought system of the ego, I teach myself—as well as my brother—that the impossible has occurred, that I have successfully separated from God, and hence can only make a choice that is filled with fear. Everything I see outside is a picture of what I believe to be true about myself inside. If I see or experience something I dislike or that upsets me in any way, it is because I have seen a mirror image of something I dislike about myself. How can a Child of God be deserving of anything but love? In choosing with the ego's lens, I keep away the one thing I long for the most: the Love of God.

If someone is behaving in a way that can be interpreted as coming from the ego rather than from the Holy Spirit, I know that they are coming from a place of fear and are themselves calling for love. How can I but forgive that behaviour, knowing that we are of one mind and that what I see outside is a reflection of what is inside my own mind? To condemn, to judge or to attack what I see in others is to condemn, to judge and to attack what I secretly believe to be true about myself. By forgiving what seems to occur before me is to forgive myself. When I forgive what another seems to have done, I do not reinforce their ego-driven behaviour, and they, too, become healed. This is the only true win-win formula.

When unsure of the correctness, or the right-mindedness, of my response in a given situation, I generally assume that I have chosen with the ego. I know that my mind is spring-loaded, in fact, hard-wired, to think with the ego's wrong-minded thought system of specialness and differences. Whenever there is uncertainty, there is lack of peace. Where there is lack of peace, there is no doubt ego involvement. To think with the right mind does not result in conflict, doubt or uncertainty. To think with the right mind leads to an experience of peace. If I have not checked with the Holy Spirit, or with Jesus, chances are that I chose with the ego. This is how we are designed. This is how we designed this world. If we were thinking with the Holy Spirit from the start, there would be no need for us to have this conversation; the world would lose the value we have given it.

> You have one test, as sure as God, by which to recognize if what you learned is true. If you are wholly free of fear of any kind, and if all those you meet or even think of you share in your perfect peace, then you can be sure that you have learned God's lesson, and not your own. Unless all this is true, there are dark lessons in your mind that hurt and hinder you, and everyone around you. The absence of perfect peace means but one thing: You think you do not will for God's Son what his

Father wills for him. Every dark lesson teaches this, in one form or another. And each bright lesson with which the Holy Spirit will replace the dark ones you do not accept, teaches you that you will with the Father and His Son. (T-14.XI.5:1–6)

What Do I Really Want?

The question that needs to be asked, at all times, if progress is to be made with this Course is, "What do I really want?" Most of us will say that we want the peace of God, that we really and truly want to return home. However, our actions belie our words. If we truly wanted the peace of God, we would have it. The Course says that we have the experience we desire. If we are having an experience of being in a dream, it is because we want this experience and we want no other. If we are having a seemingly happy dream, it is likely because the ego wants us to see the world as a safe refuge from the punishment we fear. If we are having an unhappy dream, it is because we are processing our deeply buried guilt by projecting it outwards. Any experience that depends on the dream world, or that is of the dream world, is of the ego.

I want the peace of God.

To say these words is nothing. But to mean these words is everything. If you could but mean them for just an instant, there would be no further sorrow possible for you in any form; in any place or time. Heaven would be completely given back to full awareness, memory of God entirely restored, the resurrection of all creation fully recognized. (W-pI.185.1:1–4)

To make progress with the application of the Course, the student must want to return home more than anything else in the world. Returning home to our rightful place with God must be more important than our specialness, our individuality, our foolish beliefs about ourselves and the world. Each time we pass judgment, criticize, attack or become defensive, we are choosing the ego and therefore stating that our goal is not to return home, but rather to sustain, even in a small way, our specialness. We must desire the

peace of God over being right, different, special, victimized or anything that makes our decision for separation valuable and real. We
must desire this goal so totally that no matter the circumstances,
we remember that there is another place in our mind where we can
make a different choice. Such a choice will usually lead to a more
kind and peaceful response on our part. If we are unsure about
whether we are perceiving a situation with the right mind or the
wrong mind, we can always check our peace-meter. If what we feel
is anything but a quiet, level sense of peace, any disquiet whatsoever,
then chances are that we are interpreting through the lens of judgment. And if, along the way, we should forget which way to look,
Jesus placed a few wonderful reminders for us in the Course, for
truly, he knew we would forget.

> Decision cannot be difficult. This is obvious, if you realize
> that you must already have decided not to be wholly joyous if
> that is how you feel. Therefore, the first step in the undoing
> is to recognize that you actively decided wrongly, but can as
> actively decide otherwise. Be very firm with yourself in this,
> and keep yourself fully aware that the undoing process, which
> does not come from you, is nevertheless within you because
> God placed it there. Your part is merely to return your think-
> ing to the point at which the error was made, and give it over
> to the Atonement in peace. Say this to yourself as sincerely as
> you can, remembering that the Holy Spirit will respond fully
> to your slightest invitation:
>
> *I must have decided wrongly, because I am not at peace.*
> *I made the decision myself, but I can also decide otherwise.*
> *I want to decide otherwise, because I want to be at peace.*
> *I do not feel guilty, because the Holy Spirit will undo all the*
> *consequences of my wrong decision if I will let Him.*
> *I choose to let Him, by allowing Him to decide for God for me.*
> (T-5.VII.6:1–11)

A Joyful Journey

What I have learned is that the quickest—and easiest—way out of the desert is to accept the hand of Love that reaches out to us from beyond the dunes of desolation and to be willing to look, without judgment, at a meaningless world that is not my true home. I have need of my oasis in the desert a little while longer, and that's okay. The fear of accepting the Love of God is still great. And that's okay. The lessons offered in my script provide me with opportunities to choose, and it is in learning to choose with the right mind that I will awaken slowly from the dream. Each time I look at my brothers without judgment, our dream roles fade, allowing the light of Truth to shine through. As I continue with my journey, it is with the joy and peace of knowing that with each forgiving thought, the desert grows smaller and our true home with God draws nearer.

> Forget not once this journey is begun the end is certain. Doubt along the way will come and go and go to come again. Yet is the ending sure. No one can fail to do what God appointed him to do. When you forget, remember that you walk with Him and with His Word upon your heart. Who could despair when hope like this is his? Illusions of despair may seem to come, but learn how not to be deceived by them. Behind each one there is reality and there is God. Why would you wait for this and trade it for illusions, when His Love is but an instant farther on the road where all illusions end? The end *is* sure and guaranteed by God. (C-ep.1:1–10)

Leaving the Desert

To leave the desert
Is to recognize my true self as spirit
To leave the desert
Is to know that life is eternal
To leave the desert
Is to follow the light out of the darkness
To leave the desert
Is to truly want peace
To leave the desert
Is to want, above all else, to return Home
To leave the desert
Is to forgive my brother for what he has not done
To leave the desert
Is to forgive myself for my childish choices
To leave the desert
Is to look without judgment
To leave the desert
Is to see my brother innocent
To leave the desert
Is to recognize my own innocence
To leave the desert
Is to remember the other choice
To leave the desert
Is to take His hand when I feel lost
To leave the desert
Is to know the comfort of God's Love
To leave the desert
Is to experience the joy of remembering
that my brother and I have never left our Father's side.

Pauline Edward
June 2010

The dragon that wasn't

dragons await on the other side of the wall
menacing,
I am terrified.
You come to tell me the dragon
is not there;
there is no hideous beast within.
Afraid that God will destroy me
once and for all
but remember the prodigal son
his father was waiting for him
with open arms
eternal light
blocked by hatred and division
internal light
beckoning from outside this nightmare
within
shadows fall across an open tomb
stone rolled away for all time
and beyond ...

Michael J. Miller
August 2010

BIBLIOGRAPHY AND RESOURCES

All references to *A Course in Miracles* are from the Combined Volume, Third Edition, 2007. Published by the Foundation for Inner Peace, P.O. Box 598, Mill Valley, CA 94942.

Edward, Pauline. *Making Peace with God: The Journey of a COURSE IN MIRACLES Student.* Montreal, Canada: Desert Lily Publications, 2009.

———. *The Power of Time: Understanding the Cycles of Your Life's Path.* Woodbury, MN: Llewellyn Worldwide, 2007.

Lawrence, Brother. *The Practice of the Presence of God and the Spiritual Maxims.* Mineola, NY: Dover Publications, Inc., 2005.

Merton, Thomas. *The Sign of Jonas.* Orlando, FL: Harcourt Brace Jovanovich, Inc., 1976.

Osborne, Arthur. *Ramana Maharshi and the Path of Self-Knowledge.* London, U.K.: Rider and Company, 1970.

Renard, Gary R. *The Disappearance of the Universe: Straight Talk about Illusions, Past Lives, Religion, Sex, Politics and the Miracles of Forgiveness.* Carlsbad, CA: Hay House, Inc., 2004.

Shibayama, Abbot Zenkei. *A Flower Does Not Talk: Zen Essays.* Translated by Sumiko Kudo. Rutland, VT & Tokyo, Japan: Charles E. Tuttle Company, Inc., 1970.

Wapnick, Ph.D., Kenneth. *Absence from Felicity, The Story of Helen Schucman and Her Scribing of A COURSE IN MIRACLES.* Temecula, CA: The Foundation for *A Course in Miracles*, 1991.

———. *Forgiveness and Jesus: The Meeting Place of A COURSE IN MIRACLES and Christianity.* Temecula, CA: The Foundation for *A Course in Miracles*, 1994.

———. *The Journey Home: The Obstacles to Peace in A COURSE IN MIRACLES.* Temecula, CA: The Foundation for *A Course in Miracles*, 2000.

———. *The Message of A COURSE IN MIRACLES, Volumes One and Two.* Temecula, CA: The Foundation for *A Course in Miracles*, 1997.

WORKSHOPS BY KENNETH WAPNICK, PH.D.

Following is list of some of the workshops I found helpful while working on this book. All are available
from the Foundation for *A Course in Miracles.*

Asking the Holy Spirit, 2003
Be Kind, for Everyone You Meet Is Fighting a Hard Battle, 2006
The Body, An Engine of Destruction, 2007
Cause and Effect, 2004
Climbing the Ladder Home, 1996
The Companion of the Miracle, 2001
The Decision Maker: Throned Above Fate, 2007
Escape from Love: Dissociating *A Course in Miracles,* 2004
The Experience of *A Course in Miracles*, 1998
The Happy Dream, 2005
I Want the Peace of God, 1992
Jesus' Promise: "If You but Knew...", 2006
The Laws of Chaos, 1990
Learning from the Holy Spirit, 1996
Life, A Required Course, 2005
Looking with Jesus, 2004
Love: Dark Night and Living Flame, 2006
Make No Illusion Friend, 2009
The Meaning of Judgment, 1992
The Nothingness of Something, 2007
Our Earliest Memory, 2005
The Real World: Our Home Away from Home, 1990
Rules for Decision, 1993

INTERNET RESOURCES

Please visit the author's website for additional resources.
www.paulineedward.com

Buttermilk Oatmeal Muffins

2 cups rolled oats
2 cups buttermilk (can substitute with sour cream or yogourt)
3 heaping tbsp sweetener (sugar, cane sugar, fructose, Splenda)
2 eggs
½ cup vegetable oil
2 cups flour (all whole wheat or mixed: wheat, spelt, kamut, rice)
1 tsp salt
2 tsp baking powder
1 tsp baking soda
1 tsp vanilla (optional)
2 cups fruit or other add-ins (fresh or frozen blueberries, chocolate chips, raisins, cranberries, chopped apples, shredded carrots)
½ cup chopped nuts, optional, but yummy! (almonds, walnuts, macadamia, hazelnuts, coconut or whole sunflower seeds)

1. In large bowl, combine oats and buttermilk. Add sweetener, eggs and oil. Stir to mix well.
2. In a smaller bowl, blend flours, salt, baking powder and soda.
3. Add flour mixture to oat mixture, stirring to combine. Do not over stir.
4. Fold in remaining ingredients: fruit, nuts, seeds, etc.
5. Fill greased muffin tins ¾ full.
6. Bake at 400°F for 18–20 minutes.

Have fun with this recipe—experiment with flavour essences, such as coffee (great with chocolate chips), orange or almond, and spices, such as cardamom, cinnamon, cloves, nutmeg, mace, lemon and orange rind, and, one of my favourites, green tea powder.

Makes 12 jumbo or 24 regular muffins.

Choosing the Miracle
Pauline Edward
Foreword by Susan Dugan
Desert Lily Publications

"*Choosing the Miracle* is a wonderful account of the simplicity of actually "living" *A Course in Miracles*, and opens the door for dedicated students who are willing to live and walk the Truth right here, right now, today!"
—Robyn Busfield, author of *Forgiveness is the Home of Miracles*

"In *Choosing the Miracle*, Pauline Edward graciously plants yet another shimmering guidepost for her fellow Course students. By sharing the entertaining insights gleaned from her own ongoing growth with *A Course in Miracles*, Pauline Edward looks through the ceaseless lies of the ego to reveal the truth of spirit. Stay on Course by Choosing the Miracle."
—Alexander Marchand, author of *The Universe Is a Dream*

Making Peace with God
The Journey of a *Course in Miracles* Student
Pauline Edward
Desert Lily Publications

"In *Making Peace with God*, author Pauline Edward recounts her yearning for divine connection beginning in childhood and continuing through adolescence and adulthood. Readers cannot help but identify with Edward's vivid, intimate, moving accounts of her "serial adventures" in this world, and eventual plea for a better way of living through forgiveness *A Course in Miracles* style. Her ability to articulate the Course's metaphysics while applying its mind-healing principles in the classroom of her life will inspire Course students.... a must read for *Course in Miracles* students or anyone curious about its profound, mind-healing message."
—Susan Dugan, author of *Extraordinary Ordinary Forgiveness*

The Power of Time
Understanding the Cycles of Your Life's Path
Pauline Edward
Llewellyn Worldwide

"I've used numerology for nearly 30 years. This tool is accurate, exciting, and helpful. *The Power of Time* will show you how."
—Christiane Northrup, MD, author of *Women's Bodies, Women's Wisdom* and *The Wisdom of Menopause*

"A top-notch reference, one that will excite and instruct anyone about the power of numbers in your life."
—*Dell Horoscope*

Astrological Crosses in Relationships
Understanding Cardinal, Fixed and Mutable Energies
Pauline Edward
Llewellyn Worldwide

"The best book yet about the nature of cardinal, fixed, and mutable. Her readable, insightful work can help both beginning and experienced astrologers gain much understanding about life's processes. Highly recommended."
—Michael Munkasey, PMAFA, NCGR-IV

"Absolutely excellent work on the cardinal, fixed and mutable qualities of the signs. Suitable for any level of astrologer, this goes into the subject at a deeper level than I've seen before. Thought-provoking and intelligently written."
—*The Wessex Astrologer*

About the Author

Pauline Edward is an astrologer-numerologist, Certified Professional Coach, speaker and author of *Choosing the Miracle, Making Peace with God: The Journey of a* Course in Miracles Student, *The Power of Time: Understanding the Cycles of Your Life's Path* and *Astrological Crosses in Relationships*. She is the founder of A Time for Success, a consulting business specializing in Trends, Cycles and Lifestyle Planning offering consultations and workshops for individuals and businesses worldwide. She is the recipient of a Chamber of Commerce Accolades Award for excellence in business practice.

With a background in the sciences and a fascination for all things mystical, Pauline's journey has been enriched by a wide range of experiences from research in international economics, technical writing in R & D and computer training, to studies in astrology, numerology, meditation, yoga, shamanism, the Bach Flower Remedies, herbology, healing and reiki. Her lifelong quest for truth and an understanding of the meaning of life eventually led her to *A Course in Miracles*, a study that has now become an integral part of her life. When not working with clients, she can be found indulging her passions for writing, gardening or hosting dinners with family and friends.

Pauline is available for consultations, coaching, speaking engagements and workshops. For information about services, upcoming events and publications, visit her website: www.paulineedward.com.

Lightning Source UK Ltd.
Milton Keynes UK
UKOW031516120612

194251UK00006B/30/P